THE MUSIC THERAPY SOURCEBOOK

THE MUSIC THERAPY SOURCEBOOK

A Collection of Activities Categorized and Analyzed

Cecilia H. Schulberg, R.M.T. M.M.

University of Miami, Coral Gables

HUMAN SCIENCES PRESS

72 Fifth Avenue   3 Henrietta Street
NEW YORK, NY 10011 ● LONDON, WC2E 8LU

Copyright © 1981 by Human Sciences Press, Inc.
72 Fifth Avenue, New York, New York 10011

Printed in the United States of America
123456789   987654321

Library of Congress Cataloging in Publication Data

Schulberg, Cecilia H
   The music therapy sourcebook.

   Bibliography: p. 278
   Includes index.
   1. Music therapy.   I. Title.
ML3920.S3627   615.8'5154   LC80-12945
ISBN 0-89885-007-X

Dedicated to my family:
My husband, my parents, my sisters

*The poets did well to conjoin music and medicine
in Apollo, because the office of medicine is but
to tune this curious harp of man's body, and to
reduce it to harmony.*

Francis Bacon

ACKNOWLEDGMENTS

This collection of activities could not have come into being without the assistance of those persons in the music therapy field with whom I have been associated. Many of the ideas for the activities presented were shared with me by my colleagues; many were inspired by professionals in fields related to music therapy, whom I have never met, through their written work.

I would also like to express my appreciation to the following people:

To Ara Rachel, R.M.T., who was instrumental in the birth of the idea of this book;

To Maxwell Lepper, PhD, who believed in the potential of this idea becoming a book;

To Seth Schulberg, my husband, who helped make this book become possible;

To Jane Warnement, my friend and typist; and,

To Norma Fox, my editor, who made this book become a reality.

I am most indebted to all these people, who have given me the encouragement, support, and advice that have enabled me to complete this work.

CONTENTS

INTRODUCTION

This book is a collection of music therapy activities for a wide variety of populations of varying ages and abilities. As defined by the National Association for Music Therapy, Inc., in the pamphlet "Music Therapy as a Career" (1977), music therapy is

> ... the use of music in the accomplishment of therapeutic aims; the restoration, maintenance, and improvement of mental and physical health. It is the systematic application of music, as directed by the music therapist in a therapeutic environment, to bring about desirable changes in behavior. Such changes enable the individual undergoing therapy to experience a greater understanding of himself and the world about him, thereby achieving a more appropriate adjustment to society. As a member of the therapeutic team the professional music therapist participates in the analysis of individual problems and in the projection of general treatment aims before planning and carrying out specific musical activities. Periodic evaluations are made to determine the effectiveness of the procedures employed.

Other more detailed definitions may be found elsewhere (Gaston, 1968; Alvin, 1974).

However, the music therapist has no extensive single catalogue of activities, systematically categorized according to *type of activity,* with each activity analyzed according to required skills and abilities as well as goals, procedures, and so on. Other sources have allowed the limits of a given *population* to suggest the activities.

Each activity presented in this collection has been analyzed according to Avedon's model (Columbia, 1971). Carol A. Peterson (1976) presented this model in a paper she gave at Michigan State University entitled, "Activity Analysis and Prescriptive Programming: Purpose, Procedures, Applications." Avedon's model allows for the delineation of the various elements of each activity. The model provides a greater opportunity for accurate analysis by focusing on the activity itself. The ten classifications of the model furnish a further breakdown to analyze the existing constituents of each activity. These ten areas are (1) purpose of the activity, (2) procedure for action, (3) rules governing action, (4) number of required participants, (5) roles of participants, (6) results or payoff, (7) abilities and skills required for action, (8) interaction patterns (see Appendix B), (9) physical setting and environmental requirements, and (10) required equipment.

According to Peterson (1976), Avedon's model "assumes that activity analysis is not simply a procedure of placing an activity into a category; rather it indicates a necessity of analyzing activities within categories for further comprehension of the inherent qualities" (p. 4). The elements that appear to be the most useful for this purpose are "abilities and skills required for action" and "interaction patterns." The model indicates that any activity requires action in all of the three behavioral domains: cognitive, sensory motor, and affective. In addition, the model indicates that a given activity must be analyzed for interaction patterns between participant and object variables.

These analyzed music therapy activities have been presented categorically, according to type of activity, in outline form. Each category is set up as its own chapter, preceded by a short explanation of the chapter heading. The categories were ordered by the type of music therapy activities most widely used. (For example, many music therapy groups begin with some sort of relaxation exercise, whereas psychiatric musicology is mainly diagnostic and is employed mostly in special individual situations.

Some activities were not included because the basic idea behind them is covered in the discussion of another activity. For example, there are endless numbers of Orff activities and musical games. In light of the impossibility of including every variation of every music therapy activity possible, only the basic and unusual ones are included.

Often, many activities overlap and more than one is used in a session, and such instances are clearly indicated. A review of the literature appears throughout the book within the rationale of each activity category. No attempt was made to test these activities statistically with any population or age group.

Music therapists, professionals as well as students, have often been hindered in the practice of music therapy by the lack of a convenient sourcebook of activities. These activities were accumulated to provide such a sourcebook, for a wide variety of situations.

Chapter 1

MUSIC AND RELAXATION

As societies have become increasingly complex, it appears that people have become more aware of the need to relax from the tensions and pressures that arise in surviving within these societies. However, the need does not necessarily provide the knowledge. As Bonny and Savary (1973) put it,

> Many people think that relaxation means lying limp, with arms and legs flaccid and heavy. Quite the contrary: To feel relaxed is to feel weightless. Feeling weightless means that the body's muscles are in equilibrium or balance. Muscles come in pairs—one designed to push out, the other to pull back. When these muscle pairs are in balance—neither pulling nor pushing, yet ready to go either way—they are in equilibrium, and that particular part of the body feels weightless. When the muscles of the entire body are in this state of balance or weightlessness, the body is totally relaxed. (p. 23)

There are many approaches to attaining this state of total, or partial, relaxation, for example, transcendental meditation, mind control, Zen meditation, behavior modification, sleep therapy, hypnosis, and Gestalt therapy. Many approaches which have utilized music have been found to be especially effective.

One such technique, "guided imagery," has been developed by Bonny and Savary (1973). This technique helps in attaining relaxation by reaching an altered state of consciousness through music. (The method is presented in more detail in Chapter 14).

Other techniques that involve music are more active, for example, exercise to music, dance, and eurhythmics— and these are also described in more detail later. Whatever specific approach is used, the participant must *want* to relax, and although all approaches are similar in technique, not every approach will work for every person.

Since most of the other musical approaches to relaxation are presented at some point in later chapters, this chapter will deal with only one such popular therapeutic approach, *progressive relaxation training* (Bernstein & Borkover, 1973). The two men most responsible for the development of relaxation training are Edmund Jacobson (whose pioneering work led to the development of a physiological method for combating tension and anxiety in 1934) and Joseph Wolpe (who modified Jacobson's procedures, between 1948 and 1958, and applied them in a systematic program of treatment).

Relaxation training is most obviously used to relieve high-level tension responses that interfere with performance. This may include eliminating insomnia (caused by muscular tension and intrusive thoughts), aiding clients with tension-caused illnesses (such as tension headaches that have not responded to prescribed medication), and reducing tension to facilitate therapeutic communication. The tension in this last category includes less specific complaints of "general tenseness" or "tight nerves," which seem to be more related to just being awake than to any particular stimulus situation). The setting, the chair, and the dress must all provide as much comfort and support as possible. Bernstein and Borkover (1973) devised a content outline for the rational presentation of the basic procedures:

I. Introduction
    A. The procedures to be used are called progressive relaxation training.
    B. Progressive relaxation training consists of learning to tense and release various muscle groups throughout the body.
    C. An essential part of learning how to relax involves learning how to pay close attention to the feelings of tension and relaxation in your body.
    D. Learning relaxation skills is like learning other motor skills. (I will not be doing anything to you; you will simply be learning a technique.)
    E. We employ tension in order to ultimately produce relaxation.
        1. Strong tension is noticeable and you will learn to attend to these feelings.
        2. The initial production of tension gives us some "momentum" so that when we release the tension deep relaxation is the result.
    F. Questions and comments.
II. Tensing Instructions
    A. We will be dealing with sixteen muscle groups which are tensed and released. As skill develops, the number of groups will be reduced.
    B. Tensing Instructions for Arms and Hands (determine which side is dominant)
        1. Instructions for dominant hand and lower arm (make a fist)
        2. Instructions for dominant biceps (push elbow down against chair)
        3. Instructions for nondominant hand and lower arm
        4. Instructions for nondominant biceps
    C. Tensing Instructions for Face and Neck (model face-making to put client at ease)
        1. Instructions for forehead (lift eyebrows as high as possible)
        2. Instructions for central section (squint and wrinkle nose)

         3. Instructions for lower face and jaw (bite hard and pull back corners of mouth)

         4. Instructions for neck (pull chin toward chest and keep it from touching chest)

    D. Tensing Instructions for Chest and Abdomen

         1. Instructions for chest, shoulders, and upper back (pull shoulder blades together)

         2. Instructions for abdomen (make stomach hard)

    E. Tensing Instructions for Legs and Feet

         1. Instructions for dominant upper leg (counterpose top and bottom muscles)

         2. Instructions for dominant calf (pull toes toward head)

         3. Instructions for dominant foot (point and curl toes, turning foot inward)

         4. Instructions for nondominant upper leg

         5. Instructions for nondominant calf

         6. Instructions for nondominant foot

    F. Questions and answers (be sure alternative tensing strategies are determined where needed)

III. Additional Instructions

    A. Various muscle groups are going to be compared with one another in terms of depth of relaxation.

    B. Release tension immediately upon cue rather than gradually.

    C. Once a group of muscles is relaxed, do not move it unnecessarily (except to make yourself comfortable).

    D. Do not talk to me during this session. When I ask for a signal, please lift the little finger of the hand closest to me.

    E. Notification of length of session and invitation to visit rest room

    F. Removal of constraining items such as watches, rings, eyeglasses, contact lenses, and shoes

    G. Questions and comments

    H. Client reclines in chair

    I. Explanation of dimming lights (pp. 61–62)

*Reprinted from *Progressive Relaxation Training* by Douglas A. Bernstein and Thomas D. Borkovec, with permission from Research Press, Champaign, Illinois, 1973.

There are variations to these basic procedures, such as relaxation procedures for seven muscle groups, relaxation procedures for four muscle groups, relaxation through recall, relaxation by recall with counting, and relaxation by counting alone. Two of the most common applications of the basic progressive relaxation skill are "differential relaxation" and "conditioned relaxation." Differential relaxation is the more specific of the two since it involves the reduction of tension in certain muscle groups which are unnecessary for a given activity. Conditioned relaxation is a more generalized skill, enabling the client to achieve relaxation in response to a self-produced cue, and is best employed in producing nonspecific tension reduction in the face of stress. These procedures may be used with or without music.

Chapter 2

MUSIC AND SINGING

Singing is the first form of musical self-expression an individual experiences; for some, it remains the only one. It is the rare individual who cannot, or does not sing. Singing allows for a gamut of experiences that can be both motivating and liberating.

The voice is an extension of oneself, one's most intimate means of self-expression. It is a built-in musical instrument that is performed upon from birth, but which makes use of other abilities and skills as well. Perceptive, cognitive, and expressive powers are needed to work together to simultaneously produce words and melodies with meaning. The act of singing enables an individual unconsciously to integrate and organize his personality via the content and the structure of these words and melodies. And inseperable from the whole experience are his feelings about the act of himself singing and about *what* he is singing.

Within groups, singing can influence the development of social relationships. The overall responsiveness of the group to what they are singing, their mutual efforts in the performance of a song, and the feeling of belonging support each individual's personal experiences and gives them a positive social foundation.

These broad effects that singing has on the individual affect the disabled person no differently. In fact, singing has more particular effects on the disabled person, such as lessening behavioral disturbances, stimulating proper speech formation, and overcoming fears.

One such use of singing is demonstrated in "vocal dynamics" (Wasserman, 1972). Vocal dynamics "consists of speech and body exercises which assist the patient to communicate verbally and nonverbally through the use of voice, rhythm and body movement" (pp. 99–100). The focus of this approach is on using the voice and parts of the body to produce sounds and to express contrasting feelings as participants count or list such things as the letters of the alphabet and the days of the week. Body movements, which accompany the sounds, are used to reinforce the sounds and the meanings of what is said. The participants are taught to breathe deeply, which enables them to move and express themselves more freely during these simple and sequential exercises.

A technique relating to *singing therapy* is melodic intonation therapy (MIT), a method developed to assist the adult aphasic regain verbal communication (Sparks & Holland, 1976). However, melodic intonation differs from singing in that it uses only a limited range of musical notes, similar to that of a recitative. The intoned pattern is based on one of several speech prosody patterns which are reasonable choices for a given sentence, depending on the inference intended. The pattern consists of three elements: the melodic line, the rhythm, and the points of stress. Intonation patterns resembling those of well-known songs are always avoided, since regression to the words of those songs occurs if their intonation patterns are mimicked. Melodic intonation should have a slower and more lyrical tempo than speech, with more precise rhythm and more accentutated points of stress; this facilitates articulation and reduces the frequency of paraphasic errors.

Other therapeutic uses of singing are demonstrated within the activities presented in this chapter: group singing (no specific reference); group singing with discussion (no specific reference); choral singing and speaking (no specific reference); and music and signing (Gadling, 1976).

GROUP SINGING

Purpose of the Activity

To expose participants to different types of songs.
To encourage imagination and interpretive skills.
To provide for another means of verbal communication and expression.
To promote socialization via group interaction and cooperation.
To increase attention span, interest, and participation.
To provide an enjoyable and self-satisfying experience.

Procedure for Action

There are various ways to conduct this activity. New songs may be learned by rote or through the aid of printed sing-along sheets. The therapist, or one or more group members, may supply accompaniment on an instrument. Group members may simply pick songs that they know and enjoy singing.

A variation of this latter procedure is to distribute little pieces of paper, each one containing one of four well-known songs. Before distribution, the group is told to begin singing the songs as soon as they receive their papers. While they are singing, they should try to find the other group members who are singing their song and sing with them. Once everyone has found a group to sing with, the therapist or a group member may conduct the different groups in dynamics, entrances, and exits. This variation is a good prelude for singing "partner" songs and other forms of choral singing.

Other variations of group singing include singing only spontaneously suggested songs, asking nonspontaneous group members to suggest songs, agreeing with a partner on songs to sing, and choosing songs randomly from a song book.

Rules Governing Action

There are no specific rules, except in cases of variations (for example, to follow the conductor in the four-song sing-along).

Number of Required Participants

A minimum of eight is required; there is no stated maximum.

Role of Participants

To be an active participant in the singing.

Results or Payoff

Adding a new song to one's repertoire, along with the simple enjoyment of taking part in such an activity.

Abilities and Skills Required for Action

Cognitive—auditory awareness and memory.
Sensory-motor—the ability to sing.
Affective—the ability to work well with others.

Interaction Patterns

Intra-individual, aggregate, intra-group

Physical Setting and Environmental Requirements

Any setting that is comfortable and available for meeting.

Required Equipment

Nothing is actually necessary except the people themselves, but sheet music, words to the songs, instruments, a record player and records, a tape recorder and tapes, and microphones, may be useful.

GROUP SINGING WITH DISCUSSION

Purpose of the Activity

To expose participants to different types of songs.
To encourage imagination and interpretive skills.
To promote socialization via group interaction and
    cooperation.
To provide a self-satisfying and positive experience.
To provide another means of verbal communication and
    expression.
To increase attention span, interest, and participation.
To provide enjoyment.

Procedure for Action

Teach the song to the group. Have them first hear it all the way through, and then have them join in. Have the words read and discuss their meaning, as well as how the music is used to bring across the meaning of the words. This may be done to compare different types of music or periods of music, different songs by the same (or different) writers, music of different places, and so on. Instruments may also be used for accompaniment.

Rules Governing Action

There are no specific rules, although the group may decide on some.

Number of Required Participants

A minimum of two is required, but there is no stated maximum.

Roles of Participants

Everyone may take part in teaching a song, singing it, and/or discussing it with one another. In fact, everyone should be encouraged to participate as much as possible in each part.

Results or Payoff

Adding a new song to one's repertoire, along with the simple enjoyment of taking part in such an activity.

Abilities and Skills Required for Action

Cognitive—auditory awareness and memory, the ability to interpret meanings of words, the ability to express oneself.

Sensory-motor—the ability to sing, talk, and/or sign (and perhaps to clap hands, stamp feet, snap fingers, and so on, or to play rhythm and other types of instruments).

Affective—the ability to relate to others in the group.

Interaction Patterns

Intra-individual, aggregate, intra-group.

Physical Setting and Environmental Requirements

Any setting that is comfortable and available for meeting.

Required Equipment

Nothing is actually necessary except the people themselves, but sheet music, words to the songs, instruments, a
record player and records, a tape recorder and tapes, and microphones may be useful.

CHORAL SINGING AND SPEAKING

Purpose of the Activity

To promote socialization via group interaction and
   cooperation.
To expose participants to different types of choral
   pieces.
To provide another means of verbal communication
   and expression.
To increase attention span, interest, and participation.
To provide a self-satisfying and positive experience.
To provide enjoyment.

Procedure for Action

Choral singing or speaking is more advanced than group
singing, since it involves more than one melodic or speaking line
(and perhaps different words) sung simultaneously This fabric
may be built up gradually, that is, from unison to two parts, to
three, and so on. Doing rounds (such as "Row, Row, Row Your
Boat") may also help to develop choral singing or speaking.
Another variation is partner songs, that is, singing two different
songs with the same chord structure simultaneously. For example, half the group sings "When the Saints Go Marching In"
while the other half sings "Goodnight Ladies" and/or "Merrily
We Roll Along" at the same time. Sometimes it may be neces-

sary to have more than one conductor. Instruments may be used for accompaniment. The group may also prepare a presentation to sing for others.

Rules Governing Action

To follow the conductor.

Number of Required Participants

A minimum of four is required; there is no stated maximum.

Role of Participants

To sing their parts correctly.

Results or Payoff

Adding a new song to one's repertoire, being able to hold onto one's part, and the simple enjoyment of the activity.

Abilities and Skills Required for Action

Cognitive—auditory awareness and memory, having a sense of rhythm, and being able to hold onto one's part and follow the conductor.

Sensory-motor—the ability to sing and/or play an instrument.

Affective—the ability to work well with others.

Interaction Patterns

Intra-individual, aggregate, intra-group.

Physical Setting and Environmental Requirements

Any setting that is available and comfortable for meeting.

Required Equipment

Nothing is actually necessary except the people themselves, but sheet music, words to the songs, instruments, a record player and records, a tape recorder and tapes, and microphones, may be useful.

Music and Signing

Purpose of the Activity:

To provide another means of verbal communication and expression.

To promote socialization via group interaction and cooperation.

To promote perceptual-motor coordination.

To expose participants to different types of songs.

To increase attention span, interest, and participation.

To provide a self-satisfying and positive experience.

To provide enjoyment.

Procedure for Action

Teach the song to the group with the accompanying signs. "Allow the signs to flow into one another: 'paint' the atmosphere with smooth, broad strokes. Show the rhythm of the music through the swaying of the body or the signs themselves. Avoid fingerspelling, unless trying to give a special effect or emphasis. When signing as a group, experiment freely with different arrangements, e.g., signing in rounds, creating interesting visual effects with the signs, using a touch of mime, etc."

(Gadling et al., 1976). Action songs are also a variation. Have the group hear AND see the song all the way through before having them join in. (It may be necessary to teach the song in parts.) Instruments may be added later.

Rules Governing Action

To follow the conductor.

Number of Required Participants

One or more.

Role of Participants

To use the appropriate signs with the appropriate words, trying to sing and sign each song all the way through.

Results or Payoff

Adding a new song to one's repertoire, being able to express oneself manually as well as verbally, and enjoying doing this.

Abilities and Skills Required for Action

Cognitive—auditory/visual perception/memory, having a sense of rhythm, and being able to express oneself and to follow the conductor.

Sensory-motor—the ability to sing and sign simultaneously.

Affective—the ability to work well with others.

Interaction Patterns

Intra-individual, aggregate, intra-group.

Physical Setting and Environmental Requirements

Any setting that is comfortable and available for meeting.

Required Equipment

Nothing is actually necessary except the people themselves, but sheet music, words to the songs, instruments, a record player and records, a tape recorder and tapes, microphones, and projector and film or slides may be useful.

Kum Ba Yah

Kum Ba Yah is an anonymous, expressive, folk song from Africa which means "Come By Here My Lord." The verses easily lend themselves to a lead Signer singing them with the group responding "Kum Ba Yah."

Kum ba yah, my Lord,

Kum ba yah! Kum ba yah, my

(etc.)

Lord, Kum ba yah! Kum ba

yah, my Lord, Kum ba yah!

Verse 1.   Someone's   crying . . .   Verse 2.   praying . . .

Verse 3.   laughing . . .   Verse 4.   singing . . .

etc.

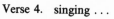

Interpretation from *Lift Up Your Hands,* used by permission, The National Grange.

Chapter 3

MUSIC AND GAMES

The World Book Encyclopedia Dictionary (1964) defines a game as "a way of playing; amusement; diversion; pastime" (p. 815). The history of games may be considered a part of the history of man as a social animal, his interrelations with other individuals and groups, his culture and civilizations, and especially his play. Throughout history, games have provided a source of amusement and excitement, intellectual stimulation and challenge, and social intercourse.

In therapy, games can provide a means of achieving therapeutic goals through the informality of the "play period." This period can be thought of as a laboratory where the participants' game skills, degree of social integration, and emotional adjustments to themselves and others can be assessed. Music provides an additional means of achieving therapeutic goals in an informal "play" atmosphere such as in "play songs" like "This Old Man." For example, almost any type of word game can employ music effectively; some examples are musical crossword puzzles, music bees, musical password, musical hangman, musical rhymes and riddles, and musical ghosts and 20 questions.

Of the endless varieties of musical games possible, only a few representative ones are presented in this chapter: musical bingo (no specific reference); musical crosswords (no specific reference); musical baseball (former colleague, 1975); musical anagrams (former colleague, 1975); musical jigsaw puzzle (former colleague, 1975); name that tune (no specific reference); musical charades (no specific reference); ball(oon) playing and music (Postl & Yaross, 1976); bean bag toss (no specific reference); and Lummi stick throwing game (former colleague, 1975).

MUSICAL BINGO

Purpose of the Activity

To increase attention span, interest, and participation.

To increase auditory awareness, perception, and recall.

To recondition word/thought associations.

To promote socialization via group interaction and cooperation.

To provide less verbal group members with an activity in which they may participate more fully.

To experience competition and develop good sportsmanship.

To stimulate academics and increase musical knowledge.

To provide enjoyment.

Procedure for Action

Special bingo cards are made with musical symbols or song titles in place of the traditional letters and numbers. Each card should contain different symbols and titles randomly placed: a "free" space in the center of the card is optional. One or two cards are distributed to each group member. If musical symbols are used, flash cards are held up and the players try to match the corresponding symbols on their cards. If song titles are used, a short segment of a song is played and the players must guess the title. If it is guessed correctly, it may be matched to the appropriate square on the cards; if guessed incorrectly, it cannot be used. Before each round, the group determines which combination wins (vertical, horizontal, diagonal or L-shaped rows, the whole card, or any of these).

Rules Governing Action

The standard rules of bingo.

Number of Required Participants

One or more

Roles of Participants

To match the symbols or titles appropriately, calling out "Bingo" when one of the combinations is satisfied. One of the group members may even be the "barker."

Results or Payoff

Depending on the group, winning may be enough; otherwise, prizes may be given to the winner of each round, to the person who wins the most rounds or points, to the person who is the most cooperative player, and so on.

Abilities and Skills Required for Action

Cognitive—auditory awareness, perception, and recall.
Sensory-motor—the ability to place chips on matching symbols or song titles and call out "Bingo."

Affective—the ability to participate competitively as a good sport.

Interaction Patterns

Intra-individual, extra-individual, aggregate, inter-individual, multilateral, intra-group.

Physical Setting and Environmental Requirements

Any setting that is comfortable and available for meeting.

Required Equipment

Bingo cards, chips, flash cards, or some means of playing song segments (such as a record player and records, a tape recorder and tapes, or a piano).

MUSICAL CROSSWORDS

Purpose of the Activity

To increase attention span, interest, and participation
To recondition word/thought associations.
To stimulate academics and increase musical knowledge.
To promote socialization via group interaction and cooperation.
To provide less verbal group members with an activity in which they may participate more fully.
To have an enjoyable and self-satisfying experience.

Procedure for Action

Charts are made with M–U–S–I–C written out at the tops of the five columns, and musical categories listed to the left vertically (Figure 3–1).

	M	*U*	*S*	*I*	*C*
Song					
Composer					
Male vocalist					
Female vocalist					
Musical show					
Instrument					

Figure 3–1.   Chart for musical crosswords.

These charts are handed out to the group members, with instructions to fill in the empty spaces appropriately, that is, first with a song that begins with the letter **M**, and so on.

The charts may be filled out individually, by small groups, or by the whole group. Completed charts may be compared and discussed. A variation of this procedure is to divide the group into teams and to set a time limit: The team who fills in the most spaces correctly wins; or the team that correctly fills in the whole chart first wins.

Rules Governing Action

There are no specific rules except for those set up by the group.

Number of Required Participants

One or more.

Roles of Participants

To correctly fill in all the blank spaces of the chart as quickly as possible.

Results or Payoff

Depending on the group, completing the chart may be enough. Otherwise, prizes may be given to the players or teams who correctly complete the chart first.

Abilities and Skills Required for Action

Cognitive—word/thought association and recall.
Sensory-motor—the ability to write.
Affective—the ability to work well in a group.

Interaction Patterns

Intra-individual, extra-individual, aggregate, inter-individual, multilateral, intra-group, inter-group.

Physical Setting and Environmental Requirements

Any setting that is comfortable and available for meeting.

Required Equipment

Charts and writing implements.

MUSICAL BASEBALL

Purpose of the Activity

To increase interest and participation in a musical setting.
To practice working in a group situation (cooperation).
To increase knowledge of music.
To have an enjoyable and self-satisfying experience.

Procedure for Action

Divide the group into two teams of equal number. (When there is not an equal number of people, someone may be chosen to be the scorekeeper.) Have each team select a captain, and assign each player on both teams a baseball position and list them on a board. From a special pack of cards that has all the plays of baseball written on them (for example, strike, ball, single to the shortstop, double to left, and home run), the batter picks a card. Unless the home run card is pulled, the person playing the position (on the team that is "on field") that the hit is going to must answer a question. The questions will pertain to areas of music that have been dealt with before in previous sessions with the group. If the answer is correct, the batter is out; if the answer is incorrect, the batter is safe. If a batter picks a home run card, the batter must answer the question. All of the rules of baseball are followed (for example, three strikes makes an out, and four balls a walk), so it may be necessary to review them before beginning.

Rules Governing Action

The official rules of baseball, reviewed beforehand.

Number of Required Participants

Minimum of 18 required, no stated maximum.

Roles of Participants

To take turns being batters and answering the questions "hit" to them.

Results or Payoff

Depending on the group, winning may be enough. Otherwise, prizes may be given to the winning team, the person who answers the most questions correctly and so on.

Abilities and Skills Required for Action

Cognitive—auditory awareness and memory, musical knowledge, and recall.

Sensory-motor—the ability to communicate with some part of the body.

Affective—the ability to take turns and to be a good sport.

Interaction Patterns

Intra-individual, inter-individual, multilateral, intra-group, inter-group.

Physical Setting and Environmental Requirements

Any setting that is comfortable and available for meeting.

Required Equipment

Blackboard and chalk, and cards made with all the baseball plays on them, and perhaps a list of questions, a record player with records, a tape recorder with tapes, and any other equipment needed to ask the questions.

MUSICAL ANAGRAMS

Purpose of the Activity

To increase attention span, interest, and participation.

To develop a positive attitude toward following directions and authority.

To promote socialization via group interaction and cooperation.

To develop good sportsmanship and stimulate academics.

To provide enjoyment.

Procedure for Action

Divide the group into two teams of equal number and hand out letters of the alphabet. (When there is not an equal number of people, someone may be chosen to be the scorekeeper.) Have each team elect a captain. The therapist then begins to ask questions about areas of music that have been dealt with before in previous sessions with the group. Each team must think of the correct answer and then, under their captains' supervision, spell it out using the letters they have. (If there are repeated letters in the answer, the team members just leave a space where the repeated letter would have been.) The first team that has the correct answer spelled out in the correct order, and then is seated, wins that round. The team captains should be changed during the course of the game.

Rules Governing Action

The number of questions and scoring should be decided beforehand, as well as any other pertinent rules that the group may deem necessary.

Number of Required Participants

Minimum of six required, no stated maximum.

Roles of Participants

To help their teams answer the questions correctly, as quickly as possible.

Results or Payoff

Depending on the group, winning may be enough. Otherwise, prizes may be given to the winning team, the team that works together most cooperatively, and so on.

Abilities and Skills Required for Action

Cognitive—auditory perception, knowledge of the material, and recall.

Sensory-motor—the ability to move into place as quickly as possible.

Affective—the ability to work well with others.

Interaction Patterns

Intra-individual, aggregate, intra-group, inter-group.

Physical Setting and Environmental Requirements

Any setting that is comfortable and available for meeting.

Required Equipment

Two sets of letters on large sheets of paper (each set having the complete alphabet), and perhaps a list of questions, a record player and records, a tape recorder and tapes, and any other equipment needed to ask the questions.

MUSICAL JIGSAW PUZZLE

Purpose of the Activity

To increase perceptual awareness.

To recondition word/thought associations.

To promote socialization via group interaction and cooperation.

To increase attention span, interest, and participation.

To provide less verbal group members with an activity in which they may participate more fully.

To promote self-esteem via a self-satisfying and positive experience.

To provide enjoyment.

Procedure for Action

Each person is given a piece of a jigsaw puzzle constructed to fit on a large card table. Each piece depicts an element found in the lyrics of a particular song. As each song is played, each person listens to discover if his or her puzzle piece is indicated. The person having the correct piece places it on the table, fitting it into the other pieces already on the table. (If there are more puzzle pieces than group members, the therapist may begin the picture with the extra pieces; there should be enough pieces for each patient to have one.) This procedure continues until the entire picture is constructed. The completed picture may then be discussed by the group.

Rules Governing Action

There are no specific rules, but the group may decide on some.

Number of Required Participants

One or more.

Results or Payoff

Having an integral part in completing the puzzle, and just the simple enjoyment of such an activity.

Abilities and Skills Required for Action

Cognitive—perceptual awareness, word/thought association, and recall.

Sensory-motor—the ability to place the puzzle piece in the correct place, and then to communicate.

Affective—the ability to work well with others.

Interaction Patterns

Intra-individual, extra-individual, aggregate, intra-group.

Physical Setting and Environmental Requirements

Any setting that is comfortable and available for meeting.

Required Equipment

A record player with records or tape recorder with tapes, and a large card-table-sized puzzle with each piece depicting an element found in the lyrics of a particular song (and enough pieces for each person to have at least one).

NAME THAT TUNE

Purpose of the Activity

To increase attention span, interest, and participation.

To promote socialization via group interaction and cooperation.

To develop a positive attitude toward authority and following directions.

To experience competition and to develop good sportsmanship.

To develop musical perception, recognition, and memory.

To have an enjoyable and self-satisfying experience.

Procedure for Action

Divide the group into two teams of equal number. (If there is an unequal number of people, someone may be chosen to be the scorekeeper.) Have each team elect a captain. A short segment of a well-known piece of music is played, and the title and composer (or recording artists if a record is used) must be named. The first team to do so correctly receives a point. If one team answers incorrectly, the other team has a chance to guess. A variation of this procedure is to name a category of songs (for example, love songs, songs about the weather, song titles with colors in them) under which the teams are to list as many songs as possible. A time limit may be used in either case.

Rules Governing Action

To encourage the teams to discuss all the possibilities and agree on one answer, only one answer should be accepted from the team captain. To encourage participation, neither team should be penalized for incorrect answers. Pertinent rules such as the number of played selections (or given categories), whether a time limit is to be set, and scoring, should be decided on beforehand by the group.

Number of Required Participants

Minimum of two required, no stated maximum.

Roles of Participants

To help their teams name as many songs correctly as quickly as possible.

Results or Payoff

Depending on the group, winning may be enough. Otherwise, prizes may be given to the winning team, the team that works most cooperatively, and so on.

Abilities and Skills Required for Action

Cognitive—auditory perception, recognition, and recall.
Sensory-motor—the ability to communicate with some part of the body.
Affective—the ability to work well with others.

Interaction Patterns

Intra-individual, inter-individual, multilateral, intra-group, inter-group.

Physical Setting and Environmental Requirements

Any setting that is comfortable and available for meeting.

Required Equipment

A record player and records, a tape recorder and tapes, or a pitch instrument on which to play the selections; blackboard and chalk, or paper and pencils.

MUSICAL CHARADES

Purpose of the Activity

To increase attention span, interest, and participation.

To promote socialization via group interaction and cooperation.

To encourage imagination in self-expression.

To promote the utilization of different body parts.

To provide a means of nonverbal communication.

To gain experience in being the focus of attention.

To experience competition and to develop good sportsmanship.

To have a positive and enjoyable experience.

Procedure for Action

Divide the group into two teams of equal number. (When there is an unequal number of people, someone may be chosen to be the scorekeeper.) Have each team elect a captain. Give a short explanation and demonstration of charades. Each member of both groups picks a song title from a list previously prepared by the therapist. It is up to the members of the teams to decide how the titles are to be acted out (by one person or more) and how to decide which team is to go first. Group members then act out the titles for their team to guess within a predetermined time limit. Variations of this procedure include doing shadow pantomime behind a lit screen; drawing illustrations as clues; pantomiming to music and having team members describe a scene using the music and the pantomime as clues.

Rules Governing Action

The standard rules of charade, for example, no words are to be used by the person pantomiming. However, these rules may be altered beforehand with the acceptance of the group; for example, sound effects may be allowed.

Number of Required Participants

Minimum of four, no stated maximum.

Roles of Participants

To take turns being mimes and to help their teams guess the correct titles.

Results or Payoff

Depending on the group, winning may be enough. Otherwise, prizes may be given to the winning team, the team that works most cooperatively, and so on.

Abilities and Skills Required for Action

Cognitive—visual perception, integration and generalization, as well as self-expression and imagination.

Sensory-motor—the ability to communicate with some part of the body and/or to draw symbolic representations.

Affective—the ability to work well with others.

Interaction Patterns

Intra-individual, extra-individual (when drawing), inter-individual, multilateral, intra-group, inter-group.

Physical Setting and Environmental Requirements

Any setting that is comfortable and available for meeting. With shadow pantomiming, the setting should be such that shadows can be made—for example, a room with blinds.

Required Equipment

Cards with song titles. Depending on the method used, a large screen or white sheet with some means of setting it up, a bright light (at least 100 watts), blackboard and chalk, a tape recorder and tapes, or a record player and records.

BALL(OON) PLAYING AND MUSIC

Purpose of the Activity

To promote perceptual-motor coordination.
To promote socialization via group interaction and cooperation.
To develop creativity and a sense of rhythm.
To increase attention span, interest, and participation.
To provide a self-satisfying and positive experience.
To provide enjoyment.

Procedure for Action

There are many musical activities that make use of a ball (or a balloon). In one, participants are seated on the floor in a semicircle. One person faces the others to keep the ball rolling, while everyone is singing the French-Canadian folksong "Roll the Ball" (see the page following this activity) and rolling the ball around the semicircle. This person begins to roll the ball to the first person on the first beat of the song. During the line "when one goes out . . . ," the next person comes to the center to keep the ball rolling. Instruments may be played for the roll of the ball. In another activity of this type, working with 6/8 pulse and meter, the following rondo may be chanted and followed with movements:

> Bounce once, bounce twice,
> Bounce the ball to someone nice.
> Bounce it high, bounce it low,
> Bounce it again to one you know.

Most of the musical activities that make use of a ball may also be played with balloons if desired.

Rules Governing Action

Following the words of the song (or chant).

Number of Required Participants

Minimum of five; no stated maximum.

Roles of Participants

To sing the song (or chant) and follow its directions.

Results or Payoff

The simple enjoyment of participating in such an activity.

Abilities and Skills Required for Action

Cognitive—auditory and visual perception and a sense of rhythm.

Sensory-motor—the ability to keep the ball rolling while singing, or to bounce the ball while chanting, to the correct rhythms.

Affective—the ability to work well with others.

Interaction Patterns

Intra-individual, aggregate, intra-group.

Physical Setting and Environmental Requirements

A large, open floor area.

Required Equipment

A large bouncing ball (or balloon), and, if wanted and available, Orff instruments. A recording entitled "Musical Ball Skills" can be ordered through Educational Activities, Inc., P.O. Box 392, Freeport, NY 11520.

Roll the Ball

French Canadian
folk song
(adapted)

Roll the ball, the ball roll on—

Roll the ball to - ge - ther.

(Six)   friends   to - ge - ther   in   a   ring —

Roll   the   ball   to - ge - ther.

When   one   goes   out   a - no- ther comes   in,

Roll   the   ball   and   watch   it   spin.

Roll   the   ball,   the   ball   roll   on—

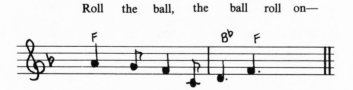

Roll   the   ball   to - ge - ther.

Bean Bag Toss

Purpose of the Activity

To promote perceptual-motor coordination.
To develop a sense of rhythmic awareness.
To reinforce awareness of right and left.
To promote socialization via group interaction and cooperation.
To have a positive and enjoyable experience.

Procedure for Action

Everyone should be seated on the floor in a circle. A bean bag should be "introduced" to the group. While singing a familiar song, such as "Row, Row, Row Your Boat," players pass the bean bag around the circle (designating right or left) to the first beat of every measure. The bag is not passed until the person who is to receive it nods his or her head on the first beat of the measure. The nodding may stop when the group seems to be able to do without it, letting each person experience the rhythm. The bean bag may also be passed on beats other than the first one of each measure; it may be tossed to anyone in the group on the same beat in each measure; it may be tossed to anyone while everyone is moving about freely; and other variations are possible.

Rules Governing Action

To be determined by the group for each variation of the activity.

Number of Required Participants

Four minimum; no stated maximum.

Roles of Participants

To pass the bean bag appropriately.

Results or Payoff

The fun of being able to pass the bean bag appropriately.

Abilities and Skills Required for Action

Cognitive—a rhythmic awareness, discrimination of left from right, perceptual awareness.

Sensory-motor—Perceptual-motor coordination of eye and hand.

Affective—the ability to be sensitive to others in working with them.

Interaction Patterns

Intra-individual, aggregate, intra-group.

Physical Setting and Environmental Requirements

A large open area.

Required Equipment

Bean bags.

LUMMI STICK THROWING GAME

Purpose of the Activity

To develop perceptual-motor coordination.
To encourage concentration and on-task behavior.

To promote socialization via group interaction and cooperation.

To provide an easy success and an enjoyable experience.

Procedure for Action

Group members are paired off with partners. Partners face each other, seated or kneeling with their seats on their heels, on the floor. Both partners grasp the ends of their separate sticks lightly, and then simultaneously throw them upright with a slight lift, across to the partner. The partners reach diagonally to catch the thrown sticks. The various movements (down, clap, pass) are demonstrated, and then each couple practices the movements individually; for example, one sequence is down, clap, pass right, down, clap, pass left. The tempo is increased and the song (or some other appropriate music) is added. The sticks should be kept rather high off the floor for easier handling.

Rules Governing Action

There are no specific rules, but the group may decide on some for a particular session.

Number of Required Participants

Minimum of two; maximum depends on the number of sticks available.

Roles of Participants

To throw one of a pair of sticks to one's partner while catching the other stick from one's partner, in various sequences of tapping the ends of the sticks on the floor, clapping, flipping, and passing the sticks—and, perhaps to sing an accompanying song later.

Results or Payoff

Having the satisfaction of being able to pass and catch the sticks successfully in the various sequences.

Abilities and Skills Required for Action

Cognitive—the ability to keep a beat.

Sensory-motor—the ability to keep a beat with parts of one's body, in various sequences of clapping, passing, catching, and flipping a pair of sticks.

Affective—the ability to work with a partner rhythmically.

Interaction Patterns

Intra-individual, aggregate, intra-group.

Physical Setting and Environmental Requirements

A large, open floor area.

Required Equipment

Pairs of Lummi sticks (approximately 14 to 18 inches long) and something to produce music with a strong beat (for example, a record player and records, a tape recorder and tapes, or percussive instruments). The Maori Stick Game may also be ordered from World Wide Games, Inc., Box 450 Delaware, OH 43015.

The Lummi stick throwing game is credited to the Maori tribe of New Zealand, as well as to a small tribe of Indians in northwest Washington. This Lummi Indian song is sung all the way through for each sequence. Each time the song is repeated, a new action is added to the former sequence. At times, the rhythms of the song and the stick throwing will not be the same.

Mä Kū ä, Kō tä ō, Ā Kū ĭ, tä nä; Mä Kū ä, Kō tä ō, Ā Kū ĭ, tä nä.

Sequences

1a. Tap ends on floor, tap together, tap right with partner.

1b. Tap ends on floor, tap together, tap left with partner.

2a. Floor, together, throw right, catch partner's left.

2b. Floor, together, throw left, catch partner's right.

3. Floor, together, throw right, throw left.

4. Floor, flip sticks, floor, together, right, left.

5. Side (right angle to body), floor, flip, (front) floor, together, right, left.

6. Side, flip, front, flip, cross sticks and tap, floor, together, right, left.

7. (Arms crossed) side, flip, (uncrossed) side, flip, front, flip, front, together, right, left.

Variations

A. Two couples play together, seated in a square. Using sequence 3, one couple starts: floor, together, right, left; the second couple starts: right, left, floor, together.

B. Players are seated in a circle. Using sequence 2a (or 2b), they throw the right stick to the left. When players become skillful, try sequence 3 in a circle (floor, together, right, left).

Chapter 4

MUSIC AND EXERCISE

The World Book Encyclopedia Dictionary (1964) defines exercise as the "repeated use of mental and physical powers to develop strength, health and energy" (p. 689). More specifically, exercise plays an essential part in maintaining one's physical and mental health by helping to increase muscle strength and flexibility, to regulate bodily processes and improve physical alignment, and to decrease tension and revitalize the body via relaxation (see Chapter 1).

Many may think that exercises must be laborious and exhausting to be beneficial. On the contrary, exercises should be challenging but not discouraging (Jones, 1976). Some movements should be rhythmic, done at a moderate tempo, but not too strenuous. Other movements should produce deliberate alternations between complete stretches of muscles and complete releases of the tautness. And other movements should distort the body so that the joints are moved through their full ranges of motion.

The length of the exercise period should be determined by

the attention spans and the physical abilities of the participants. Music is helpful in stimulating interest and providing a good rhythmic pulse. In fact, most activities in music therapy make use of exercise in an enjoyable manner, often without the participants being aware that they are actually "exercising."

This chapter deals with using music with exercise for the sake of exercise: armchair exercises (Bright, 1972); floor exercises (Findlay, 1971); exercise records (no specific reference); and tinickling sticks (former colleague, 1976).

ARMCHAIR EXERCISES

Purpose of the Activity

To encourage the utilization of different body parts.
To promote perceptual-motor movement.
To encourage concentration and on-task behavior.
To provide less verbal group members with an activity in which they may participate more fully.
To develop body orientation.
To provide an enjoyable, positive, social experience.
To develop a sense of rhythmic awareness.

Procedure for Action

There is an unlimited number of exercises that can be done seated and that do not make the participant feel that he or she is actually doing "exercises." Body movements can be coordinated to music while a person is seated, starting with the head and neck, moving down to the shoulders and arms, to the trunk and spine, and ending with the feet and legs (or in any other order), going from movement (tension) to no movement (relaxation). Action songs such as "Rock My Soul in the Bosom of

Abraham" may also be used, accompanied by clapping and arm movements. All the verses for the "Hokey Pokey" can be used except, "You put your whole self in . . ." The line "You turn yourself around" can be altered to either "wave around" (in which case a circle is drawn in the air) or "look around" (in which the head is turned from side to side). With the tune "There Is a Tavern in the Town," the following body parts can be exercised, in this order:

Head, shoulders, knees and toes, knees and toes.
Head, shoulders, knees and toes, knees and toes,
Eyes and ears and mouth and nose,
Head, shoulders, knees and toes, knees and toes.

When improvising similar songs, choose music that is so well known that thought can be concentrated on actions. For example, to the tune of "Clementine" put the words (and appropriate actions) of "Point the right hand, Then the left hand, And the right hand, Then the left" (and repeat), then "Stamp the right foot," and so on.

Rules Governing Action

To follow the leader.

Number of Required Participants

One or more.

Roles of Participants

Everyone should be encouraged to move all the appropriate body parts, staying in time with the music, singing when a song is used.

Results or Payoff

Release of tension and body development to feel better all around.

Abilities and Skills Required for Action

Cognitive—auditory-visual perception, rhythmic awareness.
Sensory-motor—perceptual-motor coordination.
Affective—the ability to work well with others.

Interaction Patterns

Intra-individual, aggregate, intra-group.

Physical Setting and Environmental Requirements

Any setting that is comfortable and available for meeting.

Required Equipment

Nothing is actually necessary except the people themselves and chairs, but a means of providing music, such as a record player or tape recorder, may be useful.

FLOOR EXERCISES

Purpose of the Activity

To encourage the utilization of different body parts.
To promote perceptual-motor coordination.
To help develop body orientation.
To provide less verbal group members with an activity in which they may participate more fully.

To promote socialization via group interaction and cooperation.

To encourage concentration and on-task behavior, imagination, and creativity.

To provide an easy successful experience that is fun and self-satisfying.

To help develop a sense of rhythmic awareness.

Procedure for Action

The important thing in this activity is not to mention the word "exercise." Let the group think they are participating in an activity involving movement or playing a game. Musical accompaniment (records, a drum, or—the most effective—improvisation on the piano) is almost a necessity, enhancing both imagination and creativity. The activity will be much more enjoyable if the exercises are presented in a creative fashion and if the group can put their imagination to use. There is an unlimited number of exercises that may be done for all parts of the body. Following are a few ideas.

All exercise sessions should begin, have intermissions, and end with relaxation exercises (see the chapter on music and relaxation). The group members may begin the activity by lying on their backs with their feet pointing toward the center of the room. On the count of one, they stretch their feet and point their toes down; on the count of two, they relax; on the count of three, they flex the muscles in their legs, so that their toes are pointed upward and their heels raised from the floor; on the count of four, they relax. Their legs should be kept straight throughout this pattern, which is repeated several times. Then, at the command of "up," they quickly sit up without the aid of their hands, their backs straight; then they slowly lower themselves to the ground, again without the aid of hands. (The therapist should hold the ankles of a group member who has trouble sitting up. If there are a significant number of group members who have difficulty, they should pair off and take turns holding ankles and sitting up). When the group feels comfortable sitting up without any aid, they may try doing so in turns, around the circle, in rhythm.

In another exercise (designed by Elsa Findlay, 1971, pp. 70–72)* the therapist may require the aid of a "magic wand" (a few colored ribbons hung on a stick) to turn the group members into a variety of animals. First, the group members are turned into horses. To achieve this, they lie on their stomachs, bend their legs back, and hold their right ankles with their right hands and their left ankles with their left hands. Then they push their legs backward and upward (so that their backs are arched) and lift their heads as high as possible. But horses tire of rocking in one position; they like to move around. So in the same position as before, but with their feet as close to their bodies as possible, they roll across the floor. (They have to roll over their hands to do this and may need some assistance). Besides rolling on the grass, horses like to stretch. So they lie on their stomachs, their hands flat on the ground under their chins and legs very straight, and lift their legs, then their heads, and then their torsos, very slowly; and, very slowly, they lower their torsos, then their heads, and then their legs.

Enough of this horsing around; the group members are now turned into frogs. They squat on their heels, their feet and knees well separated and their hands touching the ground between their knees, and they jump forward and upward in this position. For those who are capable, "leap frog" may be played, or their movements can be caught in slow motion on film. In continuous counts of four, the group members slowly rise from their squatting position, bringing their arms over their heads as they leap, and they then slowly resume their squatting position to the same number of beats—all in one continuous motion.

By this point, the group is exhausted. Turned into kittens, they go looking for a "home." To the accompaniment of a soft lullaby in 6/8 rhythm, the therapist tells the following story:

*Activities are included by permission of Elsa Findlay from *Rhythm and Movement:* Application of Dalcroze Eurhythmics. Evanston, Illinois: Summy-Birchard Company, 1971.

"The kittens were all asleep . . . " (The music continues alone until the group has relaxed and is quite still). "Then the sun came out and the kittens opened their eyes and rolled over on their backs [chord] and began to stretch one of their legs [ascending arpeggio played slowly] and then the other leg [arpeggio is repeated]. Then they stretched one arm [chord] and then the other arm [chord]. And then they sat up [chord] and rolled their heads slowly around and around [6/8 rhythm]. They looked up and down [sharp chord in the upper and then lower registers]. They looked over their right shoulder, then over their left shoulder [two sharp chords]. Then the kittens decided to go for a long, stretchy crawl." This crawl is accompanied by a slow, but vigorous rhythm. After a few minutes, the music stops abruptly. "Suddenly they stopped . . . and do you know why? . . . They'd forgotten to eat their breakfast!" (The group members scramble quickly to their "homes" as the story continues). "And there on the back porch was a bowl of milk [quiet music while the kittens lap up their milk]. When they finished their milk, they all curled up and had another nap." (The lullaby played at the beginning is repeated. As soon as the group members have relaxed into their pretended sleep, the music stops to allow for a gentle silence to fall on the room).

The group should be ready to stretch again. As elephants, they stand with their feet well apart and swing their arms (elephants' trunks) from side to side, shifting their weight as they do so. Turning from side to side, their heads follow their arm motion, and their knees flex easily as they move. (The accompaniment should stay in the 6/8 rhythm). At command, they swing a full circle to the left, followed by a sideways swing to the left, and repeat the movements to the right. A slide (♩♪♩.) , and then a hop (♩♪♩♪) , may be added. This leads them to do the "elephant walk," by taking long strides and swinging their arms in contrary motion.

The weight of each group member's body should be well over the forward foot, the arms extended in a reaching position, and the back leg should be straight. On the count of one, their arms are extended to one side; on the count of two, the forward knee is bent; on the count of three, the forward knee is bent again; on the count of four, the rear leg is pulled up to the forward leg, and they stand on tiptoe with their feet together and their arms held high over their heads.

But a storm is coming. The group members, as trees, are bending from side to side in anticipation of the storm. At first, they simply move the tips of their fingers in a gentle wind. Then their bodies begin to bend freely from side to side as the wind becomes stronger. At the climax of the storm, some of them fall. This is also accompanied by a 6/8 rhythm.*

As shown, one exercise can easily lead into another. The amount and types of exercise done vary with each group.

Rules Governing Action

To follow the commands of the therapist.

Number of Required Participants

One or more.

Roles of Participants

Everyone should be encouraged to move all the appropriate body parts in time to the music, making full use of their imaginative and creative abilities.

Results or Payoff

Release of tension and body development to make the participant feel better all round, while enjoying the process.

Abilities and Skills Required for Action

Cognitive—auditory-visual perception and a sense of rhythm.

Sensory-motor—perceptual-motor coordination.

Affective—the ability to work well with others.

Interaction Patterns

Intra-individual, aggregate, intra-group.

Physical Setting and Environmental Requirements

A large, open floor area.

Required Equipment

Some means of accompaniment, for example, records and a record player, a piano (always the most effective), or a drum.

EXERCISE RECORDS

Purpose of the Activity

To encourage the utilization of different body parts.
To promote perceptual-motor coordination.
To develop body orientation.
To provide less verbal group members with an activity in which they may participate more fully.
To promote socialization via group interaction and cooperation.
To encourage concentration and on-task behavior, imagination, and creativity.
To provide an easy successful experience which is fun and self-satisfying.
To develop a sense of rhythmic awareness.

Procedure for Action

There is an unlimited number of routines and recordings designed for different types of exercises (see Appendix A). The therapist can also devise original routines to well-known, well-liked recordings that fit the needs of specific groups.

Rules Governing Action

To follow the directions of the recording or the routine.

Number of Required Participants

One or more.

Roles of Participants

To do the routines as best as possible.

Results or Payoff

To feel physically and emotionally better in addition to enjoying the activity.

Abilities and Skills Required for Action

Cognitive—auditory perception and memory, body awareness, a sense of rhythm, and imagination and creativity.
Sensory-motor—perceptual-motor coordination.
Affective—the ability to work well with others.

Interaction Patterns

Intra-individual, aggregate, intra-group.

Physical Setting and Environmental Requirements

A large, open floor area.

Required Equipment

Records (see Appendix A) and a record player.

Tinickling Sticks

Purpose of the Activity

To improve perceptual-motor coordination.

To encourage concentration and on-task behavior.

To provide less verbal group members with an activity in which they may participate more fully.

To promote socialization via group interaction and cooperation.

To provide an easy successful experience.

To encourage creativity.

To provide enjoyment.

Procedure for Action

Two people are chosen to hold the ends of a pair of tinickling sticks. To music that has a strong beat, the people holding the sticks make rhythmic patterns with them (for example, the sticks can be held together for one beat and then separated for the next two beats). The other people in the group take turns jumping in (when the sticks are separated) and out (when the sticks are together). Wood blocks may be used beneath the ends of the sticks to make the rhythmic pulse of the sticks easier to hear and to make it easier to move the sticks together and apart. The group should be encouraged to think of variations in rhythmic patterns and ways of jumping in and out. Those who are waiting for their turns may help to keep the beat by clapping, stamping, and so on, or using rhythm instruments. More pairs of sticks may be added.

Rules Governing Action

There are no specific rules, but the group may decide on some for that session.

Number of Required Participants

Minimum of three required; no stated maximum.

Roles of Participants

Taking turns holding the sticks and jumping in and out.

Results or Payoff

Having the satisfaction of being able to jump in and out, and thinking of and being able to do variations of rhythmic patterns and jumping in and out.

Abilities and Skills Required for Action

Cognitive—the ability to keep a beat and be creative.

Sensory-motor—the ability to keep a beat with parts of one's body, to be agile (perceptual-motor coordination), and to play rhythm instruments.

Affective—the ability to take turns and work together rhythmically.

Interaction Patterns

Intra-individual, aggregate, intra-group.

Physical Setting and Environmental Requirements

A large, open floor area.

Required Equipment

Tinickling sticks (approximately 10 feet long and made of bamboo-like wood) and something to produce music with a strong beat (for example, a record player and records, a tape recorder and tapes, or instruments). "La Yenka, Tinickling" can be found (with other exercises) on the recording "4008 Elementary School Exercises to Music," which can be ordered through Hoctor Dance Records, Inc., P.O. Box 38, Waldwick, NJ 07463.

Chapter 5

MUSIC AND DANCE

Like music, dance has played an important role in our lives since the time of early man. However, again like music, dance was not established in the therapeutic field until the middle of this century. As defined by the American Dance Therapy Association (ADTA), dance therapy is the "psychotherapeutic use of movement as a process which furthers the emotional and physical integration of the individual" (Maryland/Washington, DC/Virginia ADTA Chapter's Symposium, March 14, 1975). Paralleling music therapy, dance therapy is distinguished from other forms of dance, such as dance education, by its focus on the nonverbal aspects of behavior and its use of movement as the process for—not the product of—intervention.

With adaptations to each specific population and treatment facility, some basic goals of dance therapy include (1) the development of body image, self concept, and a wider movement repertoire; (2) increased awareness of inner physiological states and their psychological counterpart, of emotional and physical tension, and of alternatives for verbal and nonverbal behavior; and (3) expression of body-mind integration, and social and ritual interaction including individual and group statements.

Although the ADTA was founded only in 1966, Marian Chace (1954; Gaston, 1968) has practiced dance therapy since 1942. A dance therapist at St. Elizabeths Hospital in Washington, DC, she established a program in dance therapy there before the association was even founded. Chace has had the longest and most continuous role in the clinical use of dance therapy, has written more about it, and has done more to further its acceptance in the health field than any other clinician. As such, her techniques, observations, and evaluations are noteworthy.

Music and dance are closely related and often difficult to separate. Most music in the world is dance music, and it is rare when a dance is performed unaccompanied by music. The use of dance in music therapy adds a dimension that can be achieved in no other way.

With these considerations in mind, the following activities are presented in this chapter: folk, square, and social dancing (no specific reference); circle dance (former colleague, 1977); maypole (former colleagues, 1977); parachute (no specific reference); creative movement (no specific reference); and mirroring (no specific reference).

Dancing

(Folk, Square, Social)

Purpose of the Activity

To encourage the utilization of different body parts.
To promote perceptual-motor coordination.
To encourage concentration and on-task behavior.

To promote socialization via group interaction and cooperation.

To develop a sense of direction (left-right discrimination) and rhythm.

To provide less verbal group members with an activity in which they may participate more fully.

To provide an enjoyable and self-satisfying experience.

To provide a new interest that can be practiced and enjoyed in the community.

Procedure for Action

The dance steps to be shown and the music to be used depend on the ability and interest of the group. To start, most groups can handle only short and easy steps and movements. Folk and square dance steps may be interchanged and modified for more use. The therapist should keep up to date with all the latest forms of social dance, and should know older ones.

When practicing, the therapist should face in the same direction as the group to help facilitate the learning of steps (so that "rights" and "lefts" correspond). Steps should be taught individually, then grouped into short segments. Likewise, the tempo of the music should be slow and then gradually increased as the steps become learned. In more modern social dancing (and even in folk and square dancing), group members should be encouraged to make up new steps to show the others. The opportunity should be given to display the learned dances at parties and in shows.

Rules Governing Action

There are no specific rules, but the group may decide on some for a particular session.

Number of Required Participants

Minimum of eight for folk and square dancing, no stated maximum; one or more for social dancing.

Roles of Participants

To learn the different steps and perhaps to improvise on them.

Results or Payoff

Having a new dance to add to one's repertoire, and the simple enjoyment of taking part in such an activity.

Abilities and Skills Required for Action

Cognitive—the ability to follow directions, auditory awareness and recall, imagination and creativity.
Sensory-motor—perceptual-motor coordination.
Affective—the ability to work well with others.

Interaction Patterns

Intra-individual, aggregate, intra-group.

Physical Setting and Environmental Requirements

A large, open floor area.

Required Equipment

Record player and records or tape recorder and tapes.

CIRCLE DANCE

Purpose of the Activity

To encourage the utilization of different body parts.

To promote perceptual-motor coordination.

To encourage concentration and on-task behavior.

To provide less verbal group members with an activity in which they may participate more fully.

To promote socialization via group interaction and cooperation.

To develop a sense of direction (left-right discrimination) and rhythm.

To provide a self-satisfying and positive experience.

To provide enjoyment.

Procedure for Action

Teach the song "She'll be Coming 'Round the Mountain." Have the group join hands and make a circle. Stretch a ribbon around the inside of the circle and have each person hold onto it with both hands. One person is chosen to stand outside the circle. The people in the circle move in one direction while this one person moves in the other direction around the outside of the circle, and everyone sings the song (using the correct pronoun—"She'll" if it is a female, and "He'll" if it is a male). When the chorus has been sung, this person on the outside of the circle chooses a partner. The group members then lift their arms and the ribbon to let the couple into the center of the circle, and then lower them again. The couple does a square dance step (for example, swing your partner, do-si-do . . .) within the circle while everyone sings about it ("She will swing her partner when she comes . . . "). When the verse has been sung, the person who was on the outside of the circle joins this circle now while the partner chosen becomes the person outside the circle. This continues until each person has had a chance to be outside the circle and as many different square dance (or other) steps or variations have been performed by the couples.

Rules Governing Action

There are no specific rules, though the group may decide on some for that session.

Number of Required Participants

Minimum of six; maximum depends on the area used.

Roles of Participants

To join in the singing and do the proper movements.

Results or Payoff

Simply the enjoyment of taking part in such an activity.

Abilities and Skills Required for Action

Cognitive—the ability to follow directions, auditory awareness and recall, imagination and creativity.
Sensory-motor—perceptual-motor coordination.
Affective—the ability to work well with others.

Interaction Patterns

Intra-individual, aggregate, intra-group.

Physical Setting and Environmental Requirements

A large, open floor area.

Required Equipment

A ribbon long enough to reach around the inside of the circle, and a record player and records or tape recorder and tapes.

MAYPOLE

Purpose of the Activity

To encourage the utilization of different body parts.
To promote perceptual-motor coordination.
To encourage concentration and on-task behavior.
To provide less verbal group members with an activity in which they may participate more fully.
To promote socialization via group interaction and cooperation.
To develop a sense of direction (left-right discrimination) and rhythm.
To provide a self-satisfying and positive experience.
To provide enjoyment.

Procedure for Action

Have each person take hold of an end of a string and spread out into a circle, with the maypole as its center. Explain what a maypole is and what is to be done with it—walking, hopping, skipping, and running around in a circle to the left, right, forwards, backwards, turning at different speeds, with an inner circle going in one direction while an outer circle goes in the other, doing allemande (moving bodies and strings or just strings). These movements are made while the dancers are holding onto the strings with one or both hands to one side, over one's head, forwards or backwards, low to the ground, at one's waist or shoulders, and so on.

These are some of the simplest moves and may be expanded into circle and folk dances, with appropriate moves added. Other, more advanced, variations include making a one-hand switch in the air, changing directions of the circle movement or of everyone's bodies (that is, moving forwards or backwards); completing a walk-squat-walk-squat sequence in time to a count; making a "ripple" effect while moving or standing still; walking into the center and then out with and without turning around; playing "follow the leader"; and assuming the walk of different animals. Strings alone may be used without the maypole. Movement patterns can be worked out with varicolored strings. All movement should be done "in time" to music.

Rules Governing Action

There are no specific rules, but the group may decide on some.

Number of Requried Participants

Minimum of two; maximum depends on the size of the maypole and the area used.

Role of the Participants

To follow the directions of the leader.

Results or Payoff

Simply the fun of taking part in such an activity.

Abilities and Skills Required for Action

Cognitive—the ability to follow directions, imagination, and creativity.

Sensory-motor—perceptual-motor coordination.
Affective—the ability to work well with others.

Interaction Patterns

Intra-individual, aggregate, intra-group.

Physical Setting and Environmental Requirements

A large open area.

Required Equipment

A maypole and strings, and a record player and records or a tape recorder and tapes.

PARACHUTE

Purpose of the Activity

To encourage the utilization of different body parts.
To improve perceptual-motor coordination.
To increase attention span, interest, and participation.
To promote socialization via group interaction and cooperation.
To develop a sense of direction (left-right discrimination) and rhythm.
To provide enjoyment.

Procedure for Action

Spread out a parachute on the floor and have everyone place themselves around its perimeter with equal distances between them. Explain what a parachute is and what is to be done with it, such as walking, hopping, skipping, or running around in a circle, to the left, right, forwards, backwards, low to the ground, at one's waist or shoulders, and so on, and variations of any or all of these to start.

These are some of the simplest moves and may be expanded into circle and folk dances, with appropriate moves added, such as allemande right-left. Other, more advanced variations include making a one-hand switch in the air, either changing the direction of the circle movement or of everyone's body, that is, moving forwards and backwards; completing a walk-squat-walk-squat sequence in time to a count; bringing the parachute up and down while moving or standing still so that it produces a "ripple" effect; walking into the center and then out, with and without turning around; sitting down and passing the parachute or making the "ripple" effect; trying to keep a ball on it while rolling it around, moving or standing still; playing "follow the leader"; assuming the walks of different animals; moving around in a circle or under the parachute; two people switching places under the parachute (or walking, dancing, or imitating an animal while others have to guess what it is) while the others try to bring the parachute down on them; calling one person to go to the center and then back out before being caught; everyone holding up the parachute with their backs to the center, while someone is chosen to go into the center and everyone else lets the parachute fall, and then turns around and tries to guess who is missing. Whenever appropriate, all movements should be done "in time" to the music.

Rules Governing Action

There are no specific rules, but the group may decide on some for that session.

Number of Required Participants

Enough to be able to hold up the parachute, but not too many to hinder movement; the number will vary with the size of the parachute and the area used.

Roles of Participants

To follow the directions of the leader.

Results or Payoff

Simply the fun of taking part in such an activity.

Abilities and Skills Required for Action

Cognitive—the ability to follow directions, self-expression, imagination, and creativity.
Sensory-motor—perceptual-motor coordination.
Affective—the ability to work well with others.

Interaction Patterns

Intra-individual, aggregate, intra-group.

Physical Setting and Environmental Requirements

A large open area.

Required Equipment

A parachute and a record player and records or tape recorder and tapes. A special recording, "Rhythmic Parachute Play," follows the procedure given and is available (with a tri-color parachute at extra cost) at Educational Activities, Inc., P.O. Box 392, Freeport, NY 11520.

CREATIVE MOVEMENT

Purpose of the Activity

To encourage imagination in self-expression.
To encourage the utilization of different body parts.
To promote perceptual-motor coordination.
To provide a means of nonverbal communication.
To make participants aware of the sound and space in their environment, and to teach them how to use it.
To aid in the development of one's body, personality, character, confidence, and sociability.
To provide enjoyment.

Procedure for Action

Before any music is played, the group may be told to move freely around the room, any way they wish, using as much space as they can without touching anyone or anything else. The person who confines himself or herself to a small space may need assistance in moving all around the room (which may be given by other, more free-moving members of the group as well as the therapist). Once everyone is given a chance to move in silence to his or her own inner tempo and rhythms, music may be added, as accompaniment or as a stimulus. Percussive music should be avoided at the beginning, since it may have a compelling drive that may be frustrating for those who cannot keep up with it.

To help develop a sensitivity to music, the qualities of the movements may be compared to the music; body noises may also be used to accompany movement. The group may also pretend to be marionettes, to mirror one another, to make up new dances, to imitate the movement of animals, to use rhythm instruments to accompany their movements, and so on.

Rules Governing Action

None.

Number of Required Participants

One or more.

Roles of Participants

Each person should be encouraged to be as creative as possible.

Results or Payoff

Simply the enjoyment of taking part in such an activity.

Abilities and Skills Required for Action

Cognitive—self-expression, imagination, and interpretation.
Sensory-motor—perceptual-motor coordination.
Affective—the ability to relate to one's feelings as well as to others.

Interaction Patterns

Intra-individual, aggregate, intra-group.

Physical Setting and Environmental Requirements

A large open floor area.

Required Equipment

Record player with records, or tape recorder with tapes, or rhythm instruments and piano.

Mirroring

Purpose of the Activity

To promote eye/ear and limb/muscle coordination and movement.

To make participants aware of the sound and space around them, and to teach them how to use it.

To encourage imagination in self-expression.

To encourage the utilization of different body parts.

To provide a means of nonverbal communication.

To aid in the development of body, personality, and sociability.

Procedure for Action

The participants are told to find partners among themselves. (When there is an odd number of people, the therapist should pair up with someone.) They are then told that one of the people in each pair is to express himself or herself in body movements to express his or her feelings and reactions to the music that will be played to the partner. During this time, the other person is to mirror the partner's movements and to try to interpret what is being communicated by them. Both persons in each pair should be given the opportunity to initiate and mirror movements. The music should vary in mood and style. Discussion could follow on what took place and if communication within pairs was successful. Also, pairs could expand into groups.

Rules Governing Action

None.

Number of Required Participants

Minimum of two required, no stated maximum.

Roles of Participants

Each person should initiate and mirror movements, and should also be encouraged to take part in any discussion held afterwards.

Results or Payoff

Simply the enjoyment of taking part in such an activity.

Abilities and Skills Required for Action

Cognitive—self-expression, imagination, and interpretation.

Sensory-motor—perceptual-motor coordination.

Affective—the ability to relate to one's feelings as well as to others'.

Interaction Patterns

Intra-individual, aggregate, intra-group.

Physical Setting and Environmental Requirements

A large open floor area.

Required Equipment

Piano, or record player with records, or tape recorder with tapes.

Chapter 6

MUSIC APPRECIATION

As defined by Apel in the *Harvard Dictionary of Music* (1969), music appreciation is "a type of musical training designed to develop the ability to listen intelligently to music" (p. 552). Although music appreciation is considered an aspect of music education (see Chapter 18), it can be effectively utilized in therapy. That is, through the development of an individual's perception of music, sessions in music appreciation can help develop an individual's perception of himself and his environment as well. An insight into oneself and one's environment is necessary to elicit any changes in behavior, a main consideration of therapy.

This chapter presents activities that utilize music appreciation in such a therapeutic manner: all kinds of music (Wolfe, Burns, Stoll, Wichmann, 1975); nature sounds (no specific reference); music as a language (Wolfe et al., 1975); questionnaire (Wolfe et al., 1975); and gifts of life (Wolfe et al., 1975).*

*Activities are included by permission of David Wolfe, from Analysis of Music Therapy Group Procedures, Golden Valley Health Center, 1975.

ALL KINDS OF MUSIC

Purpose of the Activity

To promote socialization via verbal interaction and cooperation in a group setting.

To encourage concentration, on-task behavior, and independent thinking.

To promote confidence in asserting individual opinions more freely.

To allow for the expression of differences of opinions.

To encourage less verbal group members to verbalize in a nonthreatening situation.

To provide the opportunity of discovering different ways in which music and other stimuli are perceived.

To promote listening and interpretive skills, and decision making.

To provide a positive and enjoyable experience.

Procedure for Action

There are many ways to present all kinds of music. One way is to have the group make a list of all the types of music they know (folk, classical, popular, and so on—and to discuss their similarities and differences. Then each group member selects one type of music and finds a recording that represents that category. The recordings are played, and the group discusses their opinions of the classifications of the recordings.

A variation of this procedure is to have each group member choose a recording from the same category of music; or slips of paper, each naming one type of music, can be passed out to the group members and they can be assigned to find representative examples. The playing and discussion of recordings are carried out as before.

Another approach is to have the group listen to various

types of music and to write down all the adjectives that they feel describes each piece, for example, peaceful, melancholy, lively. The lists are read and discussion is centered around the similarities and differences in opinions. Or the lists may be passed around randomly for someone else to read. (This latter method is suggested for groups in which there are members who are uncomfortable expressing their own opinions in a group). Either of the above procedures may center on just "unusual" music, such as electronic and atonal music.

In another procedure, each member is instructed to select a song or any other piece of music which he or she particularly likes and to play it for the rest of the group. During the playing of each selection, the other group members rate the piece on a scale from 1 to 5 with accompanying reasons for the rating (for example, 1—strong dislike; 2—dislike; 3—okay; 4—like it; 5—love it). The ratings are discussed. The following questions may serve as a useful guide: Did your musical selection receive as high a rating as you expected? How does this make you feel? Given another opportunity, would you make the same choice? How do you feel about the rating your selection received? Have any of you ever felt like this before? What kinds of situations bring out similar feelings? How do you handle these feelings? In the discussion of any of the procedures, the therapist should point out the many ways in which people perceive the same stimuli; that this is acceptable, since everyone is entitled to his or her own opinions; and that often misunderstandings sometimes occur as a result.

Rules Governing Action

None.

Number of Required Participants

Two or more.

Roles of Participants

To express individual opinions about the music played.

Results or Payoff

The opportunity to express individual opinions and to see how others may perceive the same stimuli differently in a non-threatening situation.

Abilities and Skills Required for Action

Cognitive—auditory perception and interpretation, and decision making.

Sensory-motor—the ability to communicate.

Affective—the ability to relate to others as well as to oneself.

Interaction Patterns

Intra-individual, aggregate, intra-group.

Physical Setting and Environmental Requirements

Any setting that is comfortable and available for meeting.

Required Equipment

A wide assortment of various types and styles of musical recordings, a record player, paper, and pencils.

Nature Sounds

Purpose of the Activity

To become more aware of the sound and space in one's environment.

To promote socialization via group interaction and cooperation.

To increase attention span, interest, and participation.

To provide the opportunity for discovering different ways in which sound and other stimuli are perceived.

To improve listening skills.

To provide a self-satisfying and enjoyable experience.

Procedure for Action

Inform the group that this activity will begin as a walk outdoors. If possible, someone in the group is given the responsibility of recording the sounds of the walk on a cassette tape recorder. The group should try to walk through as many different environments as possible—a park, the heart of a city, a zoo, and so on—and in different types of weather—rain, sunshine, wind. This may take several excursions. At the end of the walks, the tapes are played and discussion is encouraged. The therapist may also play recordings which suggest sounds of nature, such as Debussy's "La Mer", or which actually use sounds of nature, such as Messiaen's "Oiseaux Exotiques" for comparison.

Rules Governing Action

There are no specific rules, though the group may decide on some.

Number of Required Participants

One or more.

Roles of Participants

To listen for the different sounds of nature and to participate actively in the discussion.

Results or Payoff

Simply the enjoyment that may result from becoming more aware of one's environment.

Abilities and Skills Required for Action

Cognitive—auditory/visual perception and integration.
Sensory-motor—the ability to be mobile and able to communicate.
Affective—sensitivity to one's surroundings and sharing discoveries with others.

Interaction Patterns

Intra-individual, aggregate, intra-group.

Physical Setting and Environmental Requirements

As many different settings as possible.

Required Equipment

A cassette tape recorder with blank tapes, and a record player and records.

Music as a Language

Purpose of the Activity

To promote socialization via verbal interaction and cooperation within a group.

To encourage concentration and on-task behavior.

To promote listening and interpretive skills.

To promote confidence in asserting individual opinions more freely.

To provide the opportunity of discovering the different ways in which music and other stimuli are perceived.

To encourage discussion of various ways in which feelings are handled.

To provide a positive and self-satisfying experience.

Procedure for Action

There are many ways to show music as a language. It may be easier to begin with a song with lyrics and to have the group discuss how the music complements the meaning of the words. There may be various interpretations of the same song, and this should be encouraged and discussed. Because it suggests visual correlates to auditory perception, program music is the clearest form of music that tells a story without words. Accompanying these suggested visual images are usually emotional reactions as well. As the music becomes more abstract to the listener, there may be more variations in emotional reactions and interpretations of the message the music conveys. These variations should be encouraged and you should emphasize that there is no right or wrong answer.

This process may be reversed. For example, each person in the group can be given a piece of paper with the name of an emotion written on it. Without telling the rest of the group what the emotion is, each group member finds a recording (with or without words) which is felt to describe that feeling. During the playing of the recording, the group member relates an experience when he felt that way (without revealing what the emotion actually is), and the group decides from these two clues what the emotion is. If no one can guess it correctly, the name of the emotion may be shown to another group member. This person then tells of an experience which made him feel this emotion, thus providing the group with another clue. Once the correct emotion is guessed, discussion can be encouraged by having the group give reasons why certain music (with or without words) was chosen to describe certain words.

Rules Governing Action

There are no specific rules, though the group may decide on some.

Number of Required Participants

One or more.

Roles of Participants

To interpret the message of the music played.

Results or Payoff

To develop one's interpretive skills and insight, especially with relation to music, and to gain a better understanding and appreciation of one's life.

Abilities and Skills Required for Action

Cognitive—auditory perception and interpretation.
Sensory-motor—the ability to communicate.

Affective—the ability to relate to one's feelings as well as others'.

Interaction Patterns

Intra-individual, aggregate, intra-group.

Physical Setting and Environmental Requirements

Any setting that is comfortable and available for meeting.

Required Equipment

A record player and records, paper, and pencils.

QUESTIONNAIRE

Purpose of the Activity

To promote socialization via verbal interaction and cooperation in a group setting.

To encourage less verbal group members to verbalize in a nonthreatening situation.

To provide an opportunity for group members to examine their attitudes and feelings, their personal attributes, their present methods of helping themselves, and to receive feedback from others.

To encourage independent decision making, confidence, and helping oneself when "down."

To promote concentration and on-task behavior.

To provide a positive and self-satisfying experience.

Procedure for Action

Have each group member complete a self-knowledge questionnaire that consists of open-ended statements which may be finished as chosen. The answers are discussed in the group, or in smaller subgroups when the initial group is large, with an awareness of how well they can work together. After the discussion is completed, each group selects a song which they feel describes how they functioned as a group, or expresses a common group feeling. The songs are played and discussion centers on the reasons why the groups functioned as they did, and on the feelings of the individual members about their specific group. Suggestions for improved functioning to be practiced in future sessions are encouraged.

Another approach is to have each group member choose a song that tells the rest of the group something about him or her, for example about his or her job, hobby, or family, or about some aspect of personality. After the song is played, the group member explains why it was chosen. Discussion is encouraged. Or a song may be chosen which describes something about a group member which he or she would like to change or already has changed. After the song is played and the group member explains why it was chosen and how it relates to the change, discussion is focused on the steps needed to achieve this change and on how realistic the change is for this person. Or a song may be chosen which describes something a group member feels he has going for him, and this is played, explained, and discussed. (Some group members may not be aware of anything positive going for them, and it may be necessary to have the group assist these members).

An extension of this last procedure is to have each group member list all that they have at their disposal to do to help themselves when they are beginning to feel down. A song is chosen which describes one of the items on the list, and it is played, explained, and discussed; the rest of the list may be read too. A focus question for discussion may be, "Do you see these methods as escapes from the problem or as effective ways of dealing with it?"

In another procedure, the group members are asked to think about different people they admire. A song is chosen which describes one of the positive personality traits of an admired person, and it is played, explained, and discussed. The identity of the person may or may not be disclosed. An extension of this procedure is to deal with a positive attribute— confidence—in the following manner. The song "I Have Confidence" from the musical "The Sound of Music" is played, and the group is instructed to pay close attention to the words. Ideas about confidence are then discussed (what it is, why people need it, how it is gained or lost) and written on a blackboard. Then each group member chooses a song felt to express confidence and plays it for the group. Discussion of why the songs represent confidence is encouraged. Reasons may be related and compared to the ideas previously written on the blackboard; new ideas are added as they are presented. If the group is large, subgroups may be formed and the group members may work together to select a song. This procedure may be done with any concept, such as freedom, individuality, will power, and so on.

Using music to tell something about oneself is best shown, though, in an introductory exercise. Group members choose as a partner another member with whom they are not acquainted. Partners spend about 10 to 15 minutes getting acquainted with each other, discussing any aspects of their lives, such as their family, job, or hobby. Each group member then selects a song that tells the rest of the group something about his or her partner, briefly introduces the partner to the group, plays the song, and explains why it was chosen. The therapist may aid some partners in feeding questions.

Rules Governing Action

None.

Number of Required Participants

Two or more.

Roles of Participants

To become better acquainted with one another, and with oneself, through the use of music.

Results or Payoff

To develop good socialization skills and to meet people.

Abilities and Skills Required for Action

Cognitive—auditory perception and interpretation, and decision making and convergent thinking.

Sensory-motor—the ability to communicate.

Affective—the ability to relate to and work well with others, and to be self-aware.

Interaction Patterns

Intra-individual, aggregate, intra-group.

Physical Setting and Environmental Requirements

Any setting that is comfortable and available for meeting.

Required Equipment

A wide assortment of various types and styles of musical recordings, a record player, a blackboard and chalk, and paper and pencils.

An Example of a Possible Questionnaire

1. One thing I like about myself is _____ .

2. A quality I admire in others is _____ .

3. If I were to change something about myself it would be _____ .

4. When I am a stranger to a group of people I usually _____ .

5. My feeling about needing other people is _____ .

6. When I first enter a group I feel _____ .

7. When I am asked to talk in a group I _____ .

8. When people remain silent I feel _____ .

9. When someone does all the talking I _____ .

10. My attitude toward music is _____ .

11. To help myself when I am wrapped up in the "blues" I _____ .

12. If I were a record album I would title myself __ .

13. Music makes me _____ .

14. If I am forced to listen to music I do not like I .

15. People like me when I _____ .

16. Music is _____ .

Gifts of Life

Purpose of the Activity

To promote socialization via group interaction and cooperation.

To encourage the examination of aspects of life considered to be the most important.

To provide an experience in the acts of giving and receiving, and the feelings associated with them.

To promote convergent thinking.

To provide a positive and self-satisfying experience.

Procedure for Action

This is an activity to be used with a group whose members are somewhat acquainted with one another. Each member of the group writes his name on a piece of paper. The therapist collects these pieces of paper and distributes them randomly within the group. The group is then asked to imagine what they would place in a basket containing the "gifts of life," and that each person writes up a list of gifts to give to the person whose name appears on the piece of paper he has received. In addition to these "gifts of life," a song is chosen to "give" to this person as well. The group should be told to give serious consideration to the gifts of life and to the song they choose to give; that is, although the song does not have to correspond to any of the gifts on the list, both the song and the gifts should be chosen with regard to what is felt the person really needs. Each person should be given the opportunity to give and receive a song and a list of gifts. The list of gifts may be given during the playing of the recording of the song. The person receiving the list should read it aloud to the group, and should then be encouraged to comment on the gifts of life and the song given to him.

Rules Governing Action

There are no specific rules, though the group may decide on some.

Number of Required Participants

Two or more.

Roles of Participants

To construct a list of gifts of life to be given with a song to another member in the group, and to comment on the gifts and song received.

Results or Payoff

The opportunity of sharing gifts and the good feelings that come with them, and the opportunity to see how others perceive a person and to reveal these perceptions in a nonthreatening situation.

Abilities and Skills Required for Action

Cognitive—convergent thinking and recall.
Sensory-motor—the act of writing.
Affective—the ability to relate to others as well as to oneself.

Interaction Patterns

Intra-individual, aggregate, intra-group.

Physical Setting and Environmental Requirements

Any setting that is comfortable and available for meeting.

Required Equipment

A varied assortment of recordings, a record player, pieces of paper and pencils.

Chapter 7

WORKING WITH INSTRUMENTS

Due to the nature of instrumental activities, participants are required to take an active part in the production of the music and are drawn together with the other group members in the mutuality of their efforts. Nordoff and Robbins (1971) have found that "live music, which can be flexibly adapted to suit the working situation, has a greater therapeutic potential than recorded music" (p. 79). The authors also believe that the more severe the disabilities of the participants, the truer this is. Recordings are necessary to provide an array of background musical experience and a wealth of musical knowledge, but Nordoff and Robbins feel their use is limited in progressively active instrumental-musical experiences.

Regardless of the participants' musical-rhythmic capacities, each mechanical reproduction of music maintains its own tempo each time it is played. In fact, every musical element a recording contains is identically reproduced with each playing, so the participants' responses to the recording "tend to become habitual, and their playing to it automatic; the functional relationship they form to the music is limited because it becomes fundamentally mechanical. Recorded music is not addressed, cannot be addressed, directly and at the moment . . . it lacks the enlivening immediacy of human contact that the therapist, as a leader or musician, can provide" (Nordoff & Robbins, 1971, pp. 79–80).

Finding ways to open up the experience of music to the participants, and bringing them into a musical activity through the instruments they play, are ways to increase the effectiveness of instrumental activity in music therapy. The participants' abilities to play certain instruments may be limited, but the instruments can "be given genuine musical significance through the way in which they are set in an appropriate musical context" (Nordoff & Robbins, 1971, p. 82). Nordoff and Robbins maintain that each instrumental part can be set in such a way that it becomes essential to the performance of the group. And the part of each participant, with its own musical meaning, should become integrated into a total musical experience that will contain, and require, the work of all the participants. Via such experiences, participants are given the opportunities to develop perceptiveness, concentration, initiative, commitment, perseverance, responsibility, purpose, and self-confidence— central and essential qualities for the growth of integrated personalities.

Each instrument should be used so that its individual characteristics stand out clearly in performance, and its distinctive sound complements or contrasts the other instruments being played. As the musical character of an instrument becomes clearer to the participant, he can become more conscious of the part he plays, and feel its meaning and importance in the total performance of the group. He has found another means of self-expression and communication and belonging.[*]

Once instruments are introduced, they can be used effec-

[*]From Music Therapy in Special Education by Nordoff and Robbins, Copyright 1971, by John Jay Publication, Reprinted by permission of Harper and Row, Publishers, Inc.

tively in, and can often enhance, any musical activity. The following instrumental activities are presented in this chapter: autoharp (no specific reference); melodica and recorder (no specific reference); dulcimer and kalimba (no specific reference); resonator bells (no specific reference); synthesizer (no specific reference); rhythm band (no specific reference); jug band (no specific reference); and, instrumental combo (no specific reference).

AUTOHARP

Purpose of the Activity

To provide a means of nonverbal communication and expression.

To promote socialization via group interaction and cooperation.

To promote perceptual-motor coordination.

To introduce another kind of instrument.

To develop a new interest that can be used as a leisure time hobby.

To provide a self-satisfying and positive experience.

To provide enjoyment.

Procedure for Action

Introduce the autoharp, discussing its similarities with and differences from other instruments. Demonstrate the different ways it can be played (playing chords only, picking strings only, chords and strings together, and so on), using familiar tunes that everyone knows and can sing along with the autoharp accompaniment. Give each person an opportunity to play a simple two-chord song while the rest of the group sings. Show how to strum the strings with the pick and, only if necessary, when to change the chords. For those who have difficulty coordinating these actions alone, and to promote positive interaction and cooperation, have one person strum the strings and another person change the chords. (One of these people may have to be the therapist.) The autoharp has all the advantages of a guitar and is a lot easier to play. Besides being a great instrument for accompanying singing, it may also be used in an instrumental combo.

Rules Governing Action

To change the chords correctly when accompanying.

Number of Required Participants

One or more.

Roles of Participants

To strum the strings and/or change the chords.

Results or Payoff

The ability to play an instrument in a very short time, to express oneself nonverbally, and to enjoy oneself.

Abilities and Skills Required for Action

Cognitive—auditory/visual perception, as well as the ability to express and create.
Sensory-motor—perceptual-motor coordination.
Affective—the ability to work well with others.

Interaction Patterns

Intra-individual, aggregate, intra-group.

Physical Setting and Environmental Requirements

Any setting that is comfortable and available for meeting.

Required Equipment

One or more autoharps, and possibly song sheets.

MELODICA AND RECORDER

Purpose of the Activity

To promote perceptual-motor coordination.
To enhance proper use of the breathing apparatus.
To introduce another kind of instrument.
To develop a new interest that can be used as a leisure time hobby.
To promote socialization via group interaction and cooperation.
To provide a means of nonverbal communication.
To provide a self-satisfying and positive experience.
To provide enjoyment.

Procedure for Action

Introduce the melodica or recorder, discussing its similarities with and differences from other instruments. Demonstrate breathing and finger coordination. Distribute one instrument to each individual. Sharing may be necessary, encouraging interaction. Songs may be taught via sheet music or by rote. The songs should be easy enough for the members to learn as a group in one session. The therapist can help the group play together by playing along on another instrument or by saying the notes in time. If capable, the group may be led by one of its members or by no one at all. This procedure is repeated with other songs. Eventually, the group members may improvise on a pentatonic scale, as soloists or as a group with a conductor (a therapist or group member). Both instruments are helpful preludes to brass and woodwind instruments, and the melodica is a helpful introduction to keyboard instruments as well.

Rules Governing Action

To play the correct notes in time with proper fingering.

Number of Required Participants

One or more.

Roles of Participants

To attempt to play the instrument as well as possible.

Results or Payoff

The ability to play an instrument in a relatively short time, to express oneself nonverbally, and to enjoy oneself.

Abilities and Skills Required for Action

Cognitive—auditory/visual perception, as well as the ability to express and create.
Sensory-motor—perceptual-motor coordination.
Affective—the ability to work well with others.

Interaction Patterns

Intra-individual, aggregate, intra-group.

Physical Setting and Environmental Requirements

Any setting that is comfortable and available for meeting.

Required Equipment

Melodicas or recorders, and possibly sheet music.

Dulcimer and Kalimba

Purpose of the Activity

To introduce another kind of instrument.
To promote socialization via group interaction and cooperation.
To provide an enjoyable experience.

Procedure for Action

Introduce the dulcimer or kalimba, discussing its similarities with and differences from other instruments. Demonstrate how to play the instruments with a familiar folk tune that everyone knows and can sing along with the instrumental accompaniment. Pass the instruments around, allowing each person to try it individually. This is a good activity to incorporate into a music appreciation group or session.

Rules Governing Action

None.

Number of Required Participants

One or more.

Roles of Participants

To watch the demonstration and try the instruments.

Results or Payoff

Exposure to interesting instruments, and enjoyment.

Abilities and Skills Required for Action

Cognitive—auditory/visual perception.
Sensory-motor—perceptual-motor coordination.
Affective—the ability to relate to others.

Interaction Patterns

Intra-individual, aggregate, intra-group.

Physical Setting and Environmental Requirements

Any setting that is comfortable and available for meeting.

Required Equipment

Dulcimers and kalimbas, and possibly song sheets.

RESONATOR BELLS (OR TONE BARS)

Purpose of the Activity

To promote perceptual-motor coordination.
To promote socialization via group interaction and cooperation.
To provide a means of nonverbal communication and expression.
To introduce another kind of instrument.
To provide a self-satisfying and positive experience.
To provide enjoyment.

Procedure for Action

Introduce the resonator bells (or tone bars), discussing their similarities with and differences from other instruments. Hand out at least one bell and mallet to each person, instructing in its use and making sure that each person knows what letter he or she has. Direct their attention to a chart with the letters (notes) of a song written out on it. Explain that the person who has the note (letter) being pointed to is to strike that bell ONCE. It should be made clear that it is important for the correct note to be heard, and that there should be no "anticipated playing" because they will have to figure out what is being played and anticipated playing will prevent that. The group may also be broken up into chords. After some practice, each person may be responsible for more than one bell. Each person may also be given a chance to play a whole tune by himself or herself, or to improvise alone or with others. Tone bars are also invaluable in aiding speech therapy, especially for the hearing impaired (Bang, 1979).

Rules Governing Action ·

To play only when appropriate.

Number of Required Participants

One or more.

Roles of Participants

To play their bells when it's their turn.

Results or Payoff

Having an important role in bringing a tune "to life," expressing oneself nonverbally, and enjoying oneself.

Abilities and Skills Required for Action

Cognitive—auditory/visual perception, the ability to pay attention and follow the conductor, the ability to express oneself.

Sensory-motor—perceptual-motor coordination.

Affective—the ability to work well with others.

Interaction Patterns

Intra-individual, aggregate, intra-group.

Physical Setting and Environmental Requirements

Any setting that is comfortable and available for meeting.

Required Equipment

A set of resonator bells and charts.

SYNTHESIZER

Purpose of the Activity

To introduce another kind of instrument.

To provide a means of nonverbal communication and expression.

To provide a self-satisfying and positive experience.

To provide enjoyment.

To promote perceptual-motor coordination.

To promote socialization via group interaction and cooperation.

Procedure for Action

Introduce the synthesizer, discussing its similarities with and differences from other instruments. Demonstrate how to set up a patch, and then let each person try a different one; some may even want to make up their own patches. It may also be used for improvisation and in an instrumental combo.

Rules Governing Action

To follow the markings of the patches.

Number of Required Participants

One or more.

Roles of Participants

To set up the synthesizer according to the patches and to play.

Results or Payoff

Producing different sounds, and expressing and enjoying oneself.

Abilities and Skills Required for Action

Cognitive—auditory/visual perception, expression, and creativity.
Sensory-motor—perceptual-motor coordination.
Affective—the ability to work well with others.

Interaction Patterns

Intra-individual, aggregate, intra-group.

Physical Setting and Environmental Requirements

Any setting that is comfortable and available for meeting.

Required Equipment

A synthesizer and patches.

RHYTHM BAND

Purpose of the Activity

To promote socialization via group interaction and cooperation.

To increase attention span, interest, and participation.

To develop a sense of rhythm and musical creativity.

To promote perceptual-motor coordination.

To provide less verbal group members with an activity in which they may participate more fully.

To introduce various types of instruments.

To provide a means of nonverbal communication.

To provide a self-satisfying and enjoyable experience.

Procedure for Action

The various types of rhythm instruments are set up in front of the group. One by one the instruments are introduced, discussed, demonstrated, and distributed. There are many procedures for utilizing a rhythm band. It could be as simple as just playing to a record, or it could become more complex. The group could be divided into sections, each section member having a similar instrument. Each section is given a rhythm and asked to work together to accomplish it. When each section can play its own rhythm simultaneously with the other sections, music (a recording or an instrument played by the therapist) is added. Rhythms can range from fairly easy to very difficult. Those who have difficulty with a rhythm should clap the rhythm first.

Once the group becomes proficient with this procedure, the therapist may write an arrangement for the rhythm instruments to play with a piece of music, for example, "Stars and Stripes Forever". For this, the group will need to learn how to read some type of rhythmic notation and how to follow cues from the conductor. Measures for improvisation may be included as well. The group should have the opportunity to perform at parties and in shows.

Rules Governing Action

To be a cooperative band member.

Number of Required Participants

Three or more.

Roles of Participants

Each person should be encouraged to perform as an integral member of the band.

Results or Payoff

Being an integral part of a group production and enjoying oneself.

Abilities and Skills Required for Action

Cognitive—auditory/visual perception and creativity.
Sensory-motor—perceptual-motor coordination.
Affective—the ability to work cooperatively with others.

Interaction Patterns

Intra-individual, aggregate, intra-group.

Physical Setting and Environmental Requirements

Any setting that is comfortable and available for meeting.

Required Equipment

Rhythm band instruments: various drums, sticks, bells, triangles, maracas, tambourines, castanets, claves, cymbals, blocks, guiros, and so on, and possibly musical arrangements and other instruments, such as recorders, melodicas, and autoharps. Rhythm band instruments may be ordered from: Rhythm Band Inc., P.O. Box 126, Fort Worth, TX 76101.

Rhythm Band Song

This song would be most successfully used with children or mentally retarded individuals. The rhythm instruments are set up in front of the room. Let each group member choose an instrument, and seat the members so that the instruments are grouped. Tell the players that the song will tell them when to play, and that they are to play only when the song indicates so. Then sing the song, indicating to each group, with the words of the song and visual contact, when and how they are to play. The song may be expanded on by the group. Also, it may be necessary to discuss what dynamics are, how to employ them, and what cues to look for from the conductor to employ them.

Rhythm Band Song

To-day we have a rhy-thm band made of me and you.

We each can play all a-lone or al-to-ge-ther, too.

So, first let's play to-ge-ther.

Sound like sun-ny wea-ther.

(instruments play)

Now let's hear the tri-angles play.
   ma-ra-cas
   tam-bou-rines
   cas-ta-nets
     etc.

Say-ing what e-ever they want to say.

Now let's play to-ge-ther

Sound like stor-my wea-ther.

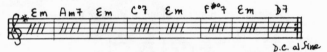

D.C. al Fine

(Alternate playing together and alone)

✳   Repeating melody line for singing alone and
◆   inserting name of instrument.
(minor)

or ★   Repeating melody line for singing together and playing
(major)   all the instruments together.

Versus: (Play major or minor depending on mood.)

Now let's play together, softly like a floating feather.

Now play sweetly like a bird, very quietly so all can
be heard.

(Additional verses may be composed by the group.)

Jug Band

Purpose of the Activity

To promote socialization via group interaction and cooperation.

To increase attention span, interest, and participation.

To develop a sense of rhythm and musical creativity.

To promote perceptual-motor coordination.

To provide less verbal group members with an activity in which they may participate more fully.

To introduce various types of instruments.

To provide a means of nonverbal communication.

To provide a self-satisfying and enjoyable experience.

Procedure for Action

The various types of instruments used to make up a jug band (washboards; bottles filled with different levels of water; pots and pans; a broom stick with a nylon string attached to it, stuck through the middle of a wash basin as a makeshift upright bass) are set up in front of the group. One by one the instruments are introduced, discussed, demonstrated, and distributed. The most widely used and most easily obtained are the water-filled bottles. The level of water determines the pitch. To produce a sound one may either blow across (not into) the top of the bottle or lightly tap the bottle with a metal object such as a spoon. Depending on the size and ability of the group, one person may play all the "water pipes" or only one bottle may be given to each person. When possible, the instruments may be obtained and assembled by the group (see Making Instruments, p. 132).

Music may be arranged by the therapist, but in such a way that the entire group has access to it and can follow it; or the performers may improvise with only a conductor (a therapist or group member) as a guide. For melody, some group members may sing, hum, or play kazoos, melodicas, recorders, or autoharps. Well-rehearsed bands should be given the opportunity to perform for others at parties or in shows.

Rules Governing Action

To be a cooperative band member.

Number of Required Participants

Four or more.

Roles of Participants

Each person should be encouraged to perform as an integral member of the band.

Results or Payoff

Being an integral part of a group production and enjoying oneself.

Abilities and Skills Required for Action

Cognitive—auditory/visual perception, as well as the ability to be creative.
Sensory-motor—perceptual-motor coordination.
Affective—the ability to work cooperatively with others.

Interaction Patterns

Intra-individual, aggregate, intra-group.

Physical Setting and Environmental Requirements

Any setting that is comfortable and available for meeting.

Required Equipment

Jug band instruments: "water pipes," washboards, one-string bass, pots and pans, harmonica, and so on, and possibly musical arrangements and other instruments such as recorders, and melodicas.

INSTRUMENTAL COMBO

Purpose of the Activity

To promote socialization via group interaction and cooperation.

To increase attention span, interest, and participation.

To develop a sense of rhythm and musical creativity.

To promote perceptual-motor coordination.

To introduce group members to various types of instruments.

To provide a means of nonverbal communication.

To provide less verbal group members with an activity in which they may participate more fully.

To provide a self-satisfying and enjoyable experience.

Procedure for Action

An instrumental combo may be made up of many different instrumental combinations, from a two-piano duo to a large orchestra, from a rock trio to a big jazz band. The type of instruments used or the number of members in the group is secondary. Of primary importance is using the instruments and the group to fulfill the goals set for the group. The musical material and abilities of the performers may be very basic or very advanced. The group should be formed according to the goals set for its members, not necessarily by the requisites usually used to form such an instrumental group. No matter what the purpose of this type of group, the following procedure may be used.

All the available instruments are set up in front of the group. One by one the instruments are introduced, discussed, demonstrated, and distributed. Explain the different approaches to using the instruments (all approaches should be feasible for that group), and describe the different sounds and effects that can be produced. Then each person should be given a chance to experiment with each instrument. The pacing of this whole procedure will vary from group to group, and may cover many sessions.

Once each member has an instrument and feels comfortable using it, have the group express their mood, feelings, or emotion through their instrument. A simple orchestration, such as a rondo, may be developed from these musical expressions, using rhythmic, speech, and movement patterns. For example, a drum may provide the basic pulse and the group may be offered a pentatonic scale for some structure and ease in initial, expressive improvisation. An "A" section may be performed by the whole group as a reoccurring chorus, while the "B" section could be a four- or eight-bar interim episode of expressive improvisation by each group member. This procedure may be used as a warm-up for practice or playing as an instrumental combo (or for any session, which may not otherwise deal with instruments at all), or it may serve as the main activity of a session.

Rules Governing Action

Only those that the group may deem necessary.

Number of Required Participants

Two or more.

Roles of Participants

Each individual should be encouraged to perform as an integral member of the group, and to be as creative as possible in self-expression.

Results or Payoff

Being an integral part of a performing group, being able to play and express oneself on an instrument, and enjoying oneself.

Abilities and Skills Required for Action

Cognitive—auditory/visual perception, creativity, and expression.

Sensory-motor—perceptual-motor coordination.

Affective—the ability to work cooperatively with others.

Interaction Patterns

Intra-individual, aggregate, inter-group.

Physical Setting and Environmental Requirements

Any setting that is comfortable and available for meeting.

Required Equipment

Instruments.

Chapter 8

MUSIC AND CREATIVITY

According to Curt Boenheim (1967), in his article "The Importance of Creativity in Contemporary Psychotherapy," creativity is

> ... a process which is characterized as a change, as some newness or originality. A new awareness being the result of the change, a greater concept of oneself and of one's goals may be produced, and such products, although not tangible as pictures or sculptures, are results or creativity. (p. 4)

Creativity may be personal (having meaning or truth only for the individual) or universal (having meaning or truth for most, if not all, of mankind). Boenheim believes that helping a patient change his outlook on life, helping him get a better image of himself and of his goals, and the relationship between that patient and his therapist are all creative. He also believes (from his work with a music therapist at the Columbus State Hospital) that music therapy, along with the other creative therapies, is an effective form of creative, therapeutic treatment, because it can utilize forms of communication without relying on verbal expression and can thus "open the door to progress."

In agreement with the definition given above, all activities of music therapy, then, involve creativity. This chapter, however, deals with the more concrete forms of creativity: composing, improvising, and sound exploration (Wolfe et al., 1975); song writing (Ficken, 1976); Haiku (former colleagues, 1975); and making instruments (Smithsonian Institution and other sources).

COMPOSING, IMPROVISING, AND SOUND EXPLORATION

Purpose of the Activity

To provide another means of nonverbal communication.

To encourage imagination and creativity.

To encourage concentration and on-task behavior.

To provide less verbal group members with an activity in which they can participate more fully.

To promote socialization via group interaction and cooperation.

To provide a positive experience.

Procedure for Action

Group members write out the letters of their full names, of phrases, and so on. These letters are matched with the letters of the music alphabet in a grid like the one shown in Figure 8–1. The resulting melody is played on a piano or xylophone (with the names of the notes taped on the keys if necessary) in any rhythm decided on by the performer. Once the "tune" is played, it may be improvised on with or without harmonization.

There are several variations of this procedure. The therapist can play the names of the group members as they per-

A	B	C	D	E	F	G
h	i	j	k	l	m	n
o	p	q	r	s	t	u
v	w	x	y	z		

Figure 8–1.   Grid for composing, improvising, and sound exploration.

formed them and can ask the group to guess whose name is being played. One group member might play his or her name, or any musical phrase, as an ostinato, while another group member plays his or her name, or any musical phrase, and improvises on it. Each group member can write a phrase about another member of the group (trying to match that person's personality with what is written about him or her), and can perform it for the group to guess who is being written about. The musical phrases can be developed into complete songs or pieces.

Rules Governing Action

Guidelines for composing.

Number of Required Participants

One or more.

Roles of Participants

Each person should be encouraged at least to "compose" his or her name, if not also to perform and improvise on it.

Results or Payoff

The satisfaction of creating something and sharing it with others.

Abilities and Skills Required for Action

Cognitive—knowledge of the alphabet, and the ability to write, create, and express.

Sensory-motor—the ability to write and play the "tunes."

Affective—the ability to relate to one's feelings, and to others' as well.

Interaction Patterns

Intra-individual, extra-individual, aggregate, intra-group.

Physical Setting and Environmental Requirements

Any setting that is comfortable and available for meeting.

Required Equipment

Any keyboard instrument and something on which to record the compositions (for example, a blackboard and chalk, a large sheet of paper and a marker, or small pieces of paper and pencils).

SONG WRITING

Purpose of the Activity

To provide another means of verbal communication.

To encourage imagination and creativity.

To encourage concentration and on-task behavior.

To provide less verbal group members with an activity in which they can participate more fully.

To promote socialization via group interaction and cooperation.

To provide a positive experience.

Procedure for Action

There are many ways to approach song writing. Following are some suggestions to facilitate the procedure.

Lyric writing should be encouraged through steps of approximation. For example, those threatened by lyric writing may substitute their own lyrics for specific words in popular songs. Whenever possible, the lyrics should be discussed, and in some cases sung, so that group members may hear the new versions of the songs and judge if the words fit the music. The next step would be to add a new verse to an existing song, or to compose a parody. As a source of aid and inspiration, the therapist could offer examples.

Concepts of lyric writing, music writing, and melody construction should be taught as simply as possible, without complex and detailed explanations. Exercises that explore natural speech pitches and rhythms should be introduced first. Orff activities help in explaining the use of the pentatonic scale, ostinati, rondo form, improvisation, and so on. The songs may also be arranged, by the group members and/or therapist, with accompaniments and voicings that help to convey the feeling the song should express. When possible, song forms, rhythmic patterns, literary devices, and other related aspects of song writing may be analyzed and put to use.

Rules Governing Action

Guidelines for song writing.

Number of Required Participants

One or more.

Roles of Participants

To progress through as many of the steps as possible toward writing a song.

Results or Payoff

The satisfaction of creating something and sharing it with others.

Abilities and Skills Required for Action

Cognitive—the ability to write, create, and express.

Sensory-motor—the ability to carry out the motions of writing.

Affective—the ability to relate to one's feelings, and to others' as well.

Interaction Patterns

Intra-individual, extra-individual, aggregate, intra-group.

Physical Setting and Environmental Requirements

Any setting that is comfortable and available for meeting.

Required Equipment

Something on which to record the songs (for example, a large sheet of paper and a marker, a blackboard and chalk, small pieces of paper and pencils, a tape recorder and tapes), a record player and records, and instruments.

HAIKU

Purpose of the Activity

To provide another means of verbal expression.

To encourage imagination and creativity.

To promote socialization via group discussion and cooperation.

To provide less verbal group members with an activity in which they may participate more fully.

To encourage concentration and on-task behavior.

To provide a positive experience.

Procedure for Action

Haiku will have to be explained to the group. It is a form of Japanese poetry utilizing 17 syllables: most typically with five syllables in the first line, seven syllables in the second line, and five syllables in the third line. This pattern can be altered to allow more freedom of expression. In haiku there are three elements, which can be in any order, to express one thought or image, for example:

Where: *On* a withered bough

What: *A crow* alone is perching

When: *Autumn evening* now.

Once the form of haiku is explained and understood, each person writes a poem.

Next the pentatonic scale is explained and demonstrated. Each person then works out a melody for his or her poem, records it (possibly with the help of the therapist or another group member), and then performs it for the rest of the group.

(Those who do not want to perform their pieces could hand them in anonymously to be performed by someone else.)

In deciding on rhythms for the compositions, the natural rhythm of the words may be used or another rhythm may be devised. Harmony, ostinatos, and pairing off with other haiku compositions, may be added. Discussion of the haiku compositions may follow the performances.

Rules Governing Action

Guidelines for writing haiku.

Number of Required Participants

One or more.

Roles of Participants

Each person should be encouraged at least to write a haiku composition (even if help is needed), if not also to perform and take part in any discussion.

Results or Payoff

The satisfaction of creating something and sharing it with others.

Abilities and Skills Required for Action

Cognitive—the abilities to express, create, and write.

Sensory-motor—the ability to write and play the compositions.

Affective—the ability to relate to one's feelings as well as others'.

Interaction Patterns

Intra-individual, extra-individual, aggregate, intra-group.

Physical Setting and Environmental Requirements

Any setting that is comfortable and available for meeting.

Required Equipment

Orff mallet instruments or other keyboard instruments on which a pentatonic scale can be devised (these may be color- or number-coded to allow easy reading, depending on the levels of the group members), and something on which to record the compositions (for example, a blackboard and chalk, a large sheet of paper and a marker, or small pieces of paper and pencils).

Examples of Haikus set to music (using black-keyed pentatonic scale)

The palm trees nearby, A-long the rim, of the shore, touch the beach softly.

wa-ter bub-bles float. On the shi-ny wa-ter, Beau-ty all a-round.

MAKING INSTRUMENTS

Purpose of the Activity

To stimulate imagination and creativity.

To promote self-esteem via the construction of a useful object.

To promote eye-hand coordination and manual dexterity.

To encourage concentration and on-task behavior.

To promote socialization via sharing and working cooperatively with others.

To provide an enjoyable experience.

Procedure for Action

Instructions for making some instruments appear on the next few pages. There are also books available on making instruments.

Rules Governing Action

To follow instructions for making the instruments and to be considerate of others sharing the same space and materials.

Number of Required Participants

One or more.

Roles of Participants

Each person should be encouraged to make as much of the instrument as possible by himself or herself.

Results or Payoff

The instruments, and possibly lessons on how to play them.

Abilities and Skills Required for Action

Cognitive—the ability to follow directions and create.
Sensory-motor—eye-hand coordination and manual dexterity.
Affective—the ability to share and work cooperatively with others.

Interaction Patterns

Intra-individual, extra-individual, aggregate, intra-group.

Physical Setting and Environmental Requirements

Any setting that is comfortable and available for meeting.

Required Equipment

Requirements vary with the instrument being made.

Papier-Mâché Maracas

Tear a half-dozen sheets of old newspaper into small pieces and put them into a large pot of hot water to soak for about 24 hours. Cook flour paste (made from laundry starch, or flour, and cold water) for 5 minutes. Shred the newspaper until it is thoroughly pulp, squeezing out excess water. Add the paste to the pulp until the mixture becomes sticky enough to push into shape. Crumble one sheet of dry newspaper into an oval shape and tie a string around its bottom. Mold the pulp around it, starting with a narrow neck and then widening the center portion by applying additional layers of the wet newspaper (but not too thickly). The outer coat of paper should be plain paper toweling or wrapping paper. Allow two to three days for drying.

Papier-mâché molded around a pencil or piece of wire hanger (or any other stick ¾ to 1-inch thick) can be used for the handle. When the body of the maraca is dried, ease out the crumbled newspaper and insert buttons, dried beans, or noodles. Insert the handle and close up any open spaces with tape or gummed paper. Papier-mâché for a smooth outer layer. Paint and shellac.

Nail Chimes

Knot large nails or spikes onto a heavy string. Remove the top and bottom of a shoebox (for the frame) and lay it on its long side. Attach each end of the string to the frame so that the nails hang down and swing freely. Use another nail to strike.

Cardboard Bell and Bottle Cap Tambourines

Place one of two paper plates on top of the other and pin tiny bells around the edges with safety pins. Or sew through two layers of cardboard with heavy cotton or elastic thread to attach bells loosely to the rim, evenly spaced around it. Then paint the cardboard. Or drive nails through two or three bottle caps and into a small piece of wood so that the bottle caps move freely against each other when the wood is moved. Paint the wood.

Shakers

Put dried rice, beans, or noodles in empty juice, soda, or beer cans, small plastic containers, and so on, and tape over the opening. Then decorate the container.

Water Chimes and Whistle

Fill empty soda bottles of the same size with different amounts of water, so that when struck on the outside, each one produces a different pitch. Blowing across the top of the bottle produces a whistling sound.

Sand Blocks

Paste strips of sandpaper onto blocks of wood or cardboard boxes. Use one to rub against another.

Banjo

Stretch different sizes of rubber bands around a box. Pluck different parts of the rubber bands for different pitches.

Nail Violin (or Harmonica)

Drive graduated sizes of nails around the rim of a round, flat piece of wood. The nails are made to vibrate with a bow made out of a stick with a piece of nylon string attached to each end.

Bolt Triangle

Tie a piece of string around the end of a large machine or carriage bolt. Hold the bolt by the string and strike it with a large nail.

Spool Castanets

Thread empty spools on a string and shake. The spools can be painted.

Drums

Cover pots, pans, or cans with plastic lids and hit with spoons or hands.

Cymbals

Two flat pot covers can be hit together.

One-String Bass

Drill two small holes, one at each end, into a broom stick. Cut a piece of fishing line about one and one-half times the size of the stick, put it through the two holes, and tie it securely. Stand the stick in a hole in the middle of a wash basin, with the open end of the basin facing the ground. To play, hold the top end of the stick with one hand while plucking the string with the other hand. Different pitches can be produced by plucking the string up and down the stick.

Paper Harmonica

Place a plain piece of unlined white paper or wax paper over the teeth of a comb. Place the papered comb between one's lips (without getting the comb wet) and hum a tune while moving one's mouth over the teeth of the comb (somewhat like playing a kazoo).

Metal Guiros

Washboards are strummed with fingernails or a metal object.

Rubber Hose Panpipes

Cut a piece of rubber shower hose five inches long. (If the hose has too much curve, straighten it in hot water). Mark off four inches on a pencil from the eraser end. Roll a piece of clay (about the size of a marble) into a cylinder shape about an inch long. Put the piece of clay into one end of the five-inch piece of hose. While holding a finger over the clay, put the marked pencil in the other end until it reaches the four-inch mark: This will be the correct length for the inside of the pipe.

The clay should fit tightly so that you cannot see through the pipe. If there is too much clay, push it out with the pencil. If there is not enough, take out the pencil and drop in little pieces of clay. When blown, this pipe will produce the pitch "G."

Other pitches are made the same way, but with different lengths of hose. For pitch "A," cut four and one-half inches of hose and mark the pencil at three and one-half inches. For pitch "B," cut three and three-quarters inches of hose and mark the pencil at three and one-third inches. To put the pipes together, place a little wad of clay between the pipes and wrap them with tape. Mark each pipe with its pitch. To produce sounds, blow across the tops of the pipes rather than down into them.

Box Harp

Glue or tape all the openings of a cardboard box measuring about 13 X 10 X 8 inches. (Boxes can be obtained free in a grocery store.) With an old ballpoint pen, punch a hole midway at the width's edge so that it goes through the other side of the box (Figure 8–2, Diagram 1). Cut a piece of fishing line about

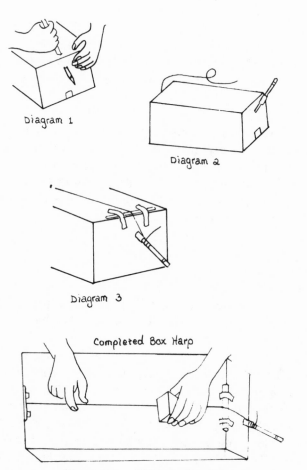

Diagram 1

Diagram 2

Diagram 3

Completed Box Harp

Figure 8–2.   Making a box harp.

twice the length of the box, put it through the two holes and tie it securely. Punch a hole at the other end of the length of the box, about two inches from the top. Wrap tape around the middle of a pencil and insert it in the hole (Figure 8–2, Diagram 2).

Wrap the fishing line around the pencil, pulling it tight so that the pencil is against the box. Tie or loop the line around the pencil so that it will not slip. Push the pencil down until the point can be pushed up into the top of the box to hold the line taut. (If the line is not tight enough, remove the pencil and loop the line around it). Put a popsicle stick (or another pencil) at each end under the fishing line so that the stick rests on the edge of the box.

Tape the stick down (Figure 8–2, Diagram 3). Cut a piece of cardboard about an inch wide and three inches long. Score in two places, equally distanced, with a blunt knife or scissor. Fold and tape to make a "bridge." Make a small notch for the string to slide against. Place the bridge under the string, moving it along the length of the box to produce different pitches while plucking the string. (See Figure 8–2.)

Gee-Haw-Whammy-Diddle

The gee-haw-whammy-diddle is a rhythm toy that makes a characteristic sound when one stick is rubbed back and forth across deep notches in another stick (Figure 8–3). A spinner nailed to one end of the serrated stick will revolve in response to the vibrations. With practice, the spinner can be made to move to the right or left at will, hence, the name "gee-haw."

Time should be kept to the music. Almost any sort of twigs or sticks can be used for making a whammy-diddle; birch dowels (available in lumber yards or hardware stores) work especially well. The rubbing stick is usually made thinner than the notched stick. Drill a hole for the spinner nail in both spinner and dowel. The spinner is just a thin, round piece of wood. The nail should fit tightly in the notched dowel, but not so tight that the dowel splits. Dimensions are not critical. (See Figure 8–3.)

Mouth Bow

The mouth (or "tune") bow is an ancient musical instrument which is still used by African Bushmen, some music makers of the Appalachian Mountains, and other people. It can

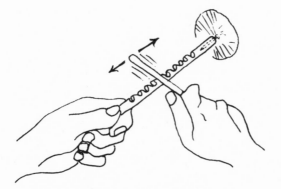

Figure 8–3.   A gee-haw-whammy-diddle.

be made from a fresh branch from a living hardwood tree (approximately three feet long with a one-inch diameter), or from a reasonably stiff yardstick (those with metal-reinforced holes at the ends are the best). For the string, use No. 7 gauge (0.018 inch) steel music wire (used for guitars, banjos, pianos, or as springs by tool and die makers). Nylon monofilament fishing line or long neck, nylon banjo string may also be used for a softer tone; however, other instrument strings are too short to be used. (If using the monofilament, get a heavy gauge one such as 60-pound test line).

Tie the string to one end of the stick. A safe bow can be made by pushing the ends into the wood (or through the holes of the yardstick) before wrapping the slack wire at each end. Bend the stick carefully before tying the other end of the string to the other end of the wood, so that the stick remains bent and the string stays very taut. The tightness of the string will determine the drone note or "tuning" of the bow. If the tone of the bow is too weak, the stick may be too limber to hold the string tight enough. Try making it more taut without breaking the stick.

To play the bow, make a small letter "O" with your lips while spreading your jaws open to make your cheeks taut at the same time. Place one end of the flat side of the bow against your

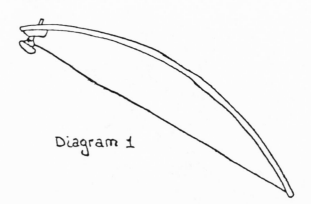

Diagram 1

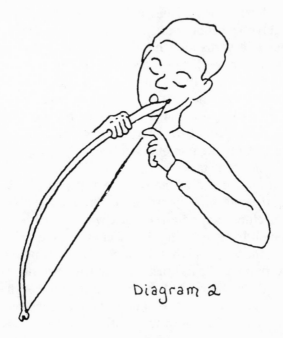

Diagram 2

Figure 8–4. A mouth bow. The type shown in Diagram 1 can be "tuned" with a violin peg.

cheek near your mouth. Pluck the string. Different pitches, or even tunes, can be played by changing the size of the "o" made by your lips while plucking the string (Figure 8–4, Diagram 2). For a bow that can be "tuned," carve or buy a violin peg and install it (Figure 8–4, Diagram 1).

Limberjacks

The limberjack is a folk toy and rhythm instrument that has been made and played in America since colonial times. It is best made of a rather hard wood that will not split easily, such as maple, black walnut, and cherry wood. Suitable pieces can usually be found as inexpensive scraps at a lumber yard. A small saw, carving knife, hand drill, and a wood file and sandpaper are needed to make the parts. A small power jig saw, if available, makes it easier to cut the variously shaped parts (Figure 8–5).

To provide a satin sheen finish, wipe on one or two coats of linseed oil after the final sanding on the wood. "Jack" can be decorated by drawing or painting on a face and clothing; some have even been fitted with doll-sized clothing. (A dress would make a "Limberjill").

Jack (or Jill) should be mounted on the end of an 18-inch stick: a 3/8-inch diameter dowel works fine. Arms can be held on with 3/4-inch nails or round-headed brass pins; the arms should swing freely. Hip and leg joints are held together by 1/8-inch hardwood dowels, which can be carved if dowels are not available. Pieces cut from round wooden toothpicks do work, but they are smaller and break with hard use. The hip dowel should fit tightly into the torso while allowing the thigh to move freely. Similarly, the knee dowel should fit snugly into the thigh part of the joint, and the lower leg-foot must swing loosely.

Jack will dance very well, and will also sit down when not in use, if each leg joint permits 180 degrees or more of move-

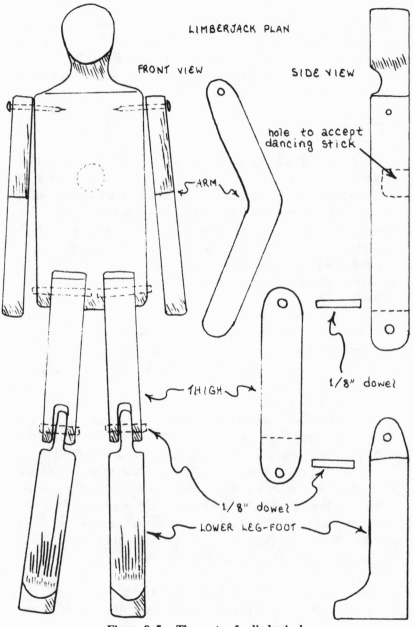

LIMBERJACK PLAN

FRONT VIEW   SIDE VIEW

hole to accept
dancing stick

← ARM →

← THIGH →

1/8" dowel

1/8" dowel

LOWER LEG-FOOT

Figure 8–5. The parts of a limberjack.

ment. Also needed is a relatively hard piece of wood, 1/8 X 3 X 24 inches, for the dancing board. To work Jack or Jill, sit on the dancing board, with as much of the board as possible sticking out beyond the chair (Figure 8–6). Hold Jack so that his feet rest on the dancing board near the far end. Bounce the board with the free hand in time to the music to make Jack tap out the rhythms.

The limberjack, mouth bow, and gee-haw-whammy-diddle are on display at the Smithsonian Institution in Washington, DC, from where these instructions were made available (Office of Public Affairs, 20560).

Figure 8–6.   Making the limberjack dance.

Chapter 9

MUSIC AND ART

According to Edith Kramer (1958), a pioneer in the development of art therapy, the main concern of the art therapist is to make available to disabled persons the "pleasures and satisfaction which creative work can give, and by insight and therapeutic skill to make such experiences meaningful and valuable to the total personality" (pp. 5–6). The art work of these individuals serves as a method of communication between them and the therapist, and is also a valuable aid in the diagnosis and evaluation of personalities. To achieve these goals the art therapist makes great use of the process of sublimation, in which the material undergoes a final transformation between the unconscious and the conscious. These transformed images are shaped into tangible pictures called art. In this way the art therapist assists in an act of integration and synthesis performed by the ego.

The main difference between music and art therapies is the *specific* medium used. The processes, goals, and even the medium (both are forms of creative expression) are very similar.

For example, the procedure of "scribbling," which was developed as a technique in art therapy, has found its way into music therapy as well (Ruppenthal, 1965). The original procedure began with "drawing" in the air with wide rhythmic movements that engaged the whole body. When a certain freedom and intensity were reached, the individual drew those movements on a large sheet of paper, working with closed eyes. The resulting "scribble" was then examined from all sides until the individual "saw" forms which suggested visual images to him. He then completed these images, using those lines that fitted his ideas and obliterating others at will, so that the completed picture usually bore little resemblance to the initial scribble.

The purposes of this procedure were to enhance freedom of body movement, to encourage freedom of expression via imagination and creativity, and to make diagnostic use of the images formed. Ruppenthal (1965) defined "scribbling" as "the utilization of a patient's creative energy at the highest level of organization he can achieve 'in comfort' amid the counterpressure of his basic human needs, his conscience, and his environment." (p. 8) This definition was derived from his application of the method of scribbling to music therapy:

> The patient is under care, because something has gone wrong with his ability to organize, and the impulse to hear sounds can be useful in this treatment only if such sounds are both within his ability to organize them and to experience the satisfaction of causes and endings at that organizational level. Toward this end, the music therapist must allow the patient, yes, may even encourage him, to "scribble" musically, and he must understand those productions as the highest level of organization the patient is capable of at the time. If the patient's "scribbling" is accepted by the therapist at his face value, the reduction of tension involved in the patient's "need to please" the therapist may make some psychic energy reserves available to the patient. His natural curiosity and desire to understand may then provide a way for the therapist to guide him to higher levels of organization.* (p. 8)

*Reprinted from the *Journal of Music Therapy* with permission of the National Association for Music Therapy, Inc.

In this chapter, music and art therapies complement one another in a continuum of activities which offer the potential for self-growth, understanding, and healing: drawing to music (no specific reference); music and poster pictures (Wolfe et al, 1975); music and slides (Wolfe et al, 1975); and pictures at an exhibition (Wolfe et al., 1975).

DRAWING TO MUSIC

Purpose of the Activity

To promote socialization via verbal interaction and cooperation within a group setting.

To provide the opportunity to discover different ways in which music and other stimuli are perceived.

To promote the confidence needed to assert individual expression more freely.

To encourage on-task behavior and creativity.

To provide a positive and enjoyable experience.

Procedure for Action

A large piece of paper is spread out on the floor. The group is instructed to make a group design, with each member drawing one continuous line that corresponds with the music being played. Contrasting musical selections are used, and one design is made for each piece of music. The designs are compared with one another and to the different pieces of music.

There are many variations to this procedure. One is to have the group look for pictures in the resulting design and to make a mural from these pictures. Another variation is to have each member draw anything (not just one continuous line) to the music, and then to compare drawings for each musical selection to see if one large group picture can be derived from the smaller individual pictures.

Rules Governing Action

When one continuous line is used, there should be no break in the line during the playing of a musical selection; a new line is begun with each piece of music.

Number of Required Participants

Two or more.

Roles of Participants

Each person should be encouraged to move freely about the paper, without worrying about bumping into another person, and to be as creative as possible, even with one line.

Results or Payoff

The opportunity to display one's creativity in a nonthreatening and enjoyable experience.

Abilities and Skills Required for Action

Cognitive—auditory/visual perception and creativity.
Sensory-motor—the ability to draw with some part of one's body.
Affective—the ability to relate to one's feelings as well as to those of others.

Interaction Patterns

Intra-individual, aggregate, intra-group.

Physical Setting and Environmental Requirements

A large floor area.

Required Equipment

A large piece of paper, drawing implements, and something on which music can be played, such as a record player with records, a tape recorder with tapes, or a piano.

MUSIC AND POSTER PICTURES

Purpose of the Activity

To promote socialization via verbal interaction and cooperation in a group setting.

To promote the confidence needed to assert individual opinions and expression more freely.

To provide the opportunity to discover different ways in which music and other stimuli are perceived.

To encourage concentration, on-task behavior, and creativity.

To provide a positive experience.

Procedure for Action

Posters displaying various situations, scenes, or emotions are randomly handed out, one to each person. The group is instructed to study and interpret the pictures given to them as they listen to a selection of music being played. Discussion is encouraged via a guideline of questions: Was the music appropriate for each poster? What are the similarities and differences among the relationships of the posters to each other and the music? A variation of this procedure is to have all the posters displayed in plain view of the entire group. Several musical selections are played and the group decides which poster matches which piece of music played and why. An additional variation is to have each group member choose a piece of music that best expresses one or more posters. Discussion should be encouraged after the playing of each musical selection.

Rules Governing Action

There are no specific rules, but the group may decide on some for a particular session.

Number of Required Participants

One or more.

Roles of Participants

Each person should be encouraged to take as active a part in the discussions as possible.

Results or Payoff

Having one's opinions listened to, and even accepted by some, as well as enjoying oneself.

Abilities and Skills Required for Action

Cognitive—auditory/visual perception and discriminatory thinking.
Sensory-motor—the ability to communicate verbally.
Affective—the ability to relate to one's feelings as well as to those of others.

Interaction Patterns

Intra-individual, aggregate, intra-group.

Physical Setting and Environmental Requirements

Any setting that is comfortable and available for meeting.

Required Equipment

Posters and music (from a record player with records, a piano, or a tape recorder with tapes).

Music and Slides

Purpose of the Activity

To promote socialization via verbal interaction and cooperation within a group setting.

To promote concentration, listening skills, and independent thinking.

To promote the confidence needed to assert individual opinions more freely.

To provide a positive experience.

Procedure for Action

Each member of the group is given a piece of paper and a pencil. The group is told that the therapist will show a slide picture while playing music that was specifically selected for that slide. For each slide, each person is to write (1) whether the music fits the slide and why; (2) what thoughts come to mind from looking at the slide and listening to the music; (3) what words might describe the music and slides. Other, similar questions are also possible. After each slide, or a set of slides, is shown in this manner, the group shares what has been written by each member. To encourage discussion, the therapist may point out common ideas, different perspectives, and so on, stressing that each comment is an individual's opinion. It would also be helpful to choose slides that are somewhat related to the lives of those in the group. An additional way to promote discussion is to choose records to accompany the slides which may be controversial (for example, Paul Simon's "Old Friends" to accompany a slide of elderly people sitting in a park). Music may be used purely as background to a slide rather than chosen for the purpose of relaying an obvious message with the slide (for example, Bach's Prelude No. 2 in c Minor as background to the slide of elderly people sitting in a park).

Rules Governing Action

There are no specific rules, but the group may decide on some for a particular session.

Number of Required Participants

One or more.

Roles of Participants

Each person should be encouraged to take as active a part in the discussion as possible.

Results or Payoff

Having one's opinions listened to, and even accepted by some, as well as enjoying oneself.

Abilities and Skills Required for Action

Cognitive—auditory/visual perception and discriminatory thinking.

Sensory-motor—the ability to communicate verbally.

Affective—the ability to relate to one's feelings as well as to those of others.

Interaction Patterns

Intra-individual, aggregate, intra-group.

Physical Setting and Environmental Requirements

Any setting where a slide projector can be set up.

Required Equipment

A slide projector, screen (wall or tagboard), selected slides, music and the means on which it is to be played (record player and records, tape recorder and tapes, piano), and paper and pencils.

PICTURES AT AN EXHIBITION

Purpose of the Activity

To promote socialization via verbal interaction and cooperation in a group setting.

To encourage concentration, on-task behavior, and independent thinking.

To promote the confidence needed to assert individual opinions and expression more freely.

To provide the opportunity to discover different ways in which music and other stimuli are perceived.

To encourage verbalization by less verbal group members via a nonthreatening activity.

To provide a positive experience.

Procedure for Action

The group is presented with introductory comments about Mussorgsky, the background of "Pictures at an Exhibition," and, possibly, the recording artist from the album cover (the Emerson, Lake, and Palmer edition is suggested). Distribute to each person a list of the titles of the pictures in random order, deleting numbers and leaving spaces between each title. Before listening to the recording, the group is advised to review the list of titles. During the recording, the group is told every time the music moves to another picture. They are told to decide which title the music illustrates and to number that title appropriately.

If there is enough time between each "picture," a short explanation should be written next to each title to give the reason that number was chosen. When time does not permit this between "pictures," the explanations should be included after listening to the entire recording. (For groups whose attention spans do not allow them to write their reasons later, stop the recording between each "picture" and do not resume playing until each person has finished writing).

It should be emphasized that there are no correct or incorrect answers. Choices of titles and the pictures are discussed. This procedure can be used with other program music (Beethoven's "Pastoral Symphony," Prokofiev's "Peter and the Wolf"), but pictures must be drawn beforehand.

Rules Governing Action

Preferably, no one should know the pictorial title of each musical segment before beginning.

Number of Required Participants

One or more.

Roles of Participants

Each person should be encouraged to number the titles appropriately and to be an active participant in the discussion following.

Results or Payoff

Having one's opinions listened to, and even accepted by some, as well as enjoying oneself.

Abilities and Skills Required for Action

Cognitive—auditory/visual perception and discriminatory thinking, as well as the ability to write.

Sensory-motor—the ability to communicate verbally and the physical ability to write.

Affective—the ability to relate to one's feelings as well as to those of others.

Interaction Patterns

Intra-individual, aggregate, intra-group.

Physical Setting and Environmental Requirements

Any setting that is comfortable and available for meeting.

Required Equipment

A record player and the recording "Pictures at an Exhibition" by Mussorgsky, program notes, and paper and pencils.

Chapter 10

MUSIC AND BIBLIOTHERAPY

The application of library material in therapy was conceived by the psychiatrist, Jack J. Leedy. As defined in Leedy's book, *Poetry Therapy* (1969), bibliotherapy is "the process of assimilating the psychosocial, sociological and aesthetic values from books into human character, personality and behavior" (p. 11). Caroline Shrodes (1960) sees bibliotherapy as "the process of interaction between the personality of the reader and imaginative literature which may engage his emotions and free them for conscious and productive use" (p. 312).

Essentially, the process lies in the interactions among the literature or film, the individual, and the facilitator. The literature or films may be: imaginative (poetry, short stories, plays, or novels); didactic or expository (used subjectively rather than intellectually); or creative writing by the patient (used to express self, not literary goal); the illiterate or handicapped person may respond verbally and the facilitator can set down the response in writing. (Further study may indicate that these latter two processes are different). The individuals who find the discussion of literature or creative writing helpful to self-understanding, growth, or healing may be children or youths, adults of all capabilities who have many ways to respond emotionally to literature, and mentally ill or addictive personalities.

The facilitator is the trained person whose role is to attend to the individual—literally, to listen with intelligence as well as with the ears, and to direct care to that individual so that the participant can discover insights into the self. The appropriate goals that fit each individual's needs determine the material to be used and the means by which the facilitator will guide the use of them. Complementary materials such as related visual images, objects, and music often help in heightening the emotional impact in order to bring about better self-awareness.

In this chapter music therapy and bibliotherapy complement one another in a continuum of activities which offer the potential for self-growth, understanding, and healing through the use of literature (or films) and music; music and quotations (Wolfe et al., 1975); stories to music (Wolfe et al., 1975); sound words (Marsh, 1970); and musical reflections (Payntor & Aston, 1970).

Music and Quotations

Purpose of the Activity

To promote socialization via verbal interaction and cooperation in a group setting.

To improve listening skills and concentration.

To encourage on-task behavior and discriminatory thinking.

To promote the confidence needed to assert individual opinions more freely.

To provide a positive experience.

Procedure for Action

This activity works best with a group that is quite verbal. A pair of quotes is placed in plain view of the group. The group is told to read them carefully and then to think about them. Then a musical selection is played which would be appropriate for either quote. The members are asked which quote they think fits the music best and why. Discussion is encouraged via guideline questions and opinions offered by the therapist, such as whether anyone agrees or disagrees with either quote, and which quote is liked the best. Several pairs of quotes may be used in one session. The members' general age and temperament can help determine how controversial the quotes may be. A variation of this procedure is to have each group member write a quote appropriate to the music.

Rules Governing Action

There are no specific rules, but the group may decide on some for a particular session.

Number of Required Participants

One or more.

Roles of Participants

Each person should be encouraged to take as active a part in the discussion as possible.

Results or Payoff

Having one's opinions listened to, and even accepted by some, as well as enjoying oneself.

Abilities and Skills Required for Action

Cognitive—auditory/visual perception and discriminatory thinking.

Sensory-motor—the ability to communicate verbally.

Affective—the ability to relate to one's feelings as well as to those of others.

Interaction Patterns

Intra-individual, aggregate, intra-group.

Physical Setting and Environmental Requirements

Any setting that is comfortable and available for meeting.

Required Equipment

Something on which the quotes are written, such as cards or a blackboard and something on which music can be played, such as a record player with records, a tape recorder with tapes, or a piano.

STORIES TO MUSIC

Purpose of the Activity

To promote socialization via verbal interaction and cooperation in a group setting.

To encourage on-task behavior and concentration, independent thinking, and creativity.

To improve listening skills and attention span.

To provide the opportunity to discover different ways in which music and other stimuli are perceived.

To provide a positive experience.

Procedure for Action

The group is told that a piece of music is to be played, and that they are to think of and write about a scene or story they feel the music is depicting. Each person's story is heard, discussed, and compared to the other stories. Program music and ballads (Gershwin's "An American in Paris," Mussorgsky's "Night on Bald Mountain," Dylan's "Nashville Skyline Rag") lend themselves well to this type of activity.

A variation of this procedure is to play segments of several different types of music, rather than one piece of music. Then each person writes about a scene in a story which corresponds to the music. Writing must cease when the music is stopped, and the papers are passed to the persons to the right. Each story segment is read silently by the person who receives it. The story is then continued by the new author, who must adjust to the new music content and style. (Or a group member may continue the story without having read the previous story segment, which is folded over; this provides for some interesting stories.) The process is continued for all the musical selections. Afterwards, the stories are read.

Rules Governing Action

If previous story segments are folded over before being passed to the next person, the persons who receive the paper should not read the folded part.

Number of Required Participants

Three or more.

Roles of Participants

Each person should be encouraged to be as creative as possible in writing a story or scene.

Results or Payoff

The opportunity to display one's creativity in a nonthreatening situation, and enjoyment.

Abilities and Skills Required for Action

Cognitive—auditory/visual perception and creativity.
Sensory-motor—the ability to communicate verbally or on paper.
Affective—the ability to relate to one's feelings as well as to those of others.

Interaction Patterns

Intra-individual, aggregate, intra-group.

Physical Setting and Environmental Requirements

Any setting that is comfortable and available for meeting.

Required Equipment

Something on which music can be played—such as a record player with records, a tape recorder with tapes, or a piano—and paper and writing implements.

SOUND WORDS

Purpose of the Activity

To promote socialization via verbal interaction and cooperation in a group setting.
To promote awareness and encourage use of the aural and visual stimuli in one's environment.

To provide the opportunity to discover different ways in which sound and other stimuli are perceived.

To promote imagination and creativity.

To encourage on-task behavior and participation.

To provide enjoyment.

Procedure for Action

An onomatopoeic poem is read to the group. The group is then asked to suggest sounds that might be substituted for certain words in the poem. All ideas are tried, and combinations of sounds are eventually substituted for all the onomatopoeic words in the poem.

This idea can be expanded by arranging the poem in choric speech style. The group is divided into multipitched voices, and even soloists may be used. Changes in dynamics and tempo are especially effective. A program of several such poems and stories may be prepared for outside presentation, accentuated by dramatization, props, puppetry, and so on.

Rules Governing Action

There are no specific rules, but the group may decide on some.

Number of Required Participants

One or more.

Roles of Participants

Each person should be encouraged to contribute to the list of sounds that might be possible substitutes for certain words in the poem, and then to take part in the performance of the poem with the substitutions.

Results or Payoff

Being an integral part of a performance and having fun.

Abilities and Skills Required for Action

Cognitive—auditory/visual perception, discriminatory thinking, and imagination and creativity.

Sensory-motor—the ability to speak and to produce sounds with parts of one's body and other objects.

Affective—the ability to work well with others.

Interaction Patterns

Intra-individual, aggregate, intra-group.

Physical Setting and Environmental Requirements

Any setting that is comfortable and available for meeting.

Required Equipment

Onomatopoeic poems or stories and objects for producing substitute sounds for certain words.

MUSICAL REFLECTIONS

Purpose of the Activity

To promote socialization via verbal interaction and cooperation in a group setting.

To promote awareness and encourage use of the aural and visual stimuli in one's environment.

To provide the opportunity to discover different ways in which sound and other stimuli are perceived.

To promote concentration, on-task behavior, imagination, and creativity.

To promote the confidence needed for verbal self-expression.

To provide a positive experience.

Procedure for Action

Have the group (or smaller subgroups if the initial group is large) note all the reflections they can find, for example, in mirrors, puddles, polished surfaces, windows, and distorted mirrors at an amusement park. From this list, the group is to discuss any situations, people, or stories that come to mind when thinking of any of these reflections. Have the group members write a single or individual pieces of poetry or prose about reflections. Note that there should be no cluttering detail, that only the best ideas should be used, and that this piece should convey thoughts and feelings and some sense of the reflective nature of the mirrored objects.

For the completed work, have the group find appropriate music to accompany it—music that will create an atmosphere to exemplify the words conveying the reflected nature of the mirrored objects. The music is played as the piece of poetry or prose is read. Several such works may be produced for outside presentation. Discussion of all works should be encouraged.

Rules Governing Action

There are no specific rules, but the group may decide on some for a particular session.

Number of Required Participants

One or more.

Roles of Participants

Each person should actively contribute to the list of reflections, the writing of the piece, and the choosing of the appropriate music; there will also be group representatives who read the pieces written.

Results or Payoff

The opportunity for verbal self-expression in a nonthreatening situation, and enjoyment.

Abilities and Skills Required for Action

Cognitive—auditory/visual perception, imagination, and creativity and recall.

Sensory-motor—the ability to communicate verbally or on paper.

Affective—the ability to relate to one's feelings as well as to those of others.

Interaction Patterns

Intra-individual, aggregate, intra-group.

Physical Setting and Environmental Requirements

Any setting that is comfortable and available for meeting.

Required Equipment

Paper and writing implements, a varied collection of music to choose for the works, and a record player.

Chapter 11

MUSIC AND DRAMA

Psychodrama, a term coined by Dr. J. L. Moreno from the Greek words "psyche," meaning "mind" or "soul," and "dram," meaning "to do" or "to act", is a form of psychotherapy in which the participants enact, or re-enact, situations that have emotional significance to them. It is usually a group activity—though in certain cases the " group" may consist only of the patient and the therapist—and it is best carried out in a theater specially designed to facilitate certain therapeutic techniques.

Here is the process: One or more patients act out on the stage their "private personalities" and the personalities of other people in their lives, under the guidance of a director/therapist, and in the presence of an audience composed of other patients. When the main subject feels that another person in the scene is out of character, he may step out of his own role to show how he feels that person really does behave by temporarily taking that role himself. Any member of the audience may become part of the action on stage, either spontaneously or at the request of an actor on stage or the director.

In the course of a session, members of the group (the actors, the audience, and even the director) gain insights into their own personalities, into some of their own problems, into their own psychological workings, and into their own feelings and those of others (unless they deliberately cut themselves off from what is going on around them). Each person who acts out parts of his life on a psychodramatic stage becomes better understood in some measure, and acquires a deeper understanding of himself and others; as a result, he can direct more of his emotional energy toward finding satisfactory solutions to his daily problems, thereby relieving some of his tensions and anxieties.

In *Psychodramatic Rules, Techniques and Adjunctive Method,* Zerka T. Moreno (1966) has drawn up a list of rules that are considered necessary to follow in a psychodrama session:

I.   The subject (patient, client, protagonist) acts out his conflicts, instead of talking about them.

II. The subject or patient acts 'in the here and now,' regardless of when the actual incident took place, past, present, or future, or when the imagined incident was fantasized, or when the crucial situation out of which this present enactment arose, occurred.

III. The subject must act out 'his truth,' as he feels and perceives it, in a completely subjective manner (no matter how distorted this appears to the spectator).

IV. The patient is encouraged to maximize all expression, action, and verbal communication, rather than to reduce it.

V.   The warming up process proceeds from the periphery to the center.

VI. Whenever possible, the protagonist will pick the time, the place, the scene, the auxillary ego he requires in the production of his psychodrama.

VII. Psychodrama is just as much a method of restraint as it is a method of expression.

VIII. The patient is permitted to be as unspontaneous or inexpressive as he is at this time.

IX. Interpretation and insight-giving in psychodrama is of a different nature from the verbal types of psychotherapy.

X. Even when interpretation is given, action is primary. There can be no interpretation without previous action.

XI. Warming up to psychodrama may proceed differently from culture to culture and appropriate changes in the application of the method may have to be made.

XII. Psychodrama sessions consist of three portions: the warm up, the action portion and the post-action sharing by the group.

XIII. The protagonist should never be left with the impression that he is all alone with this type of problem in the group.

XIV. The protagonist must learn to take the role of all of those with whom he is meaningfully related, to experience those persons in his social atom, their relationship to him and to one another.

XV. The director must trust the psychodrama method as the final arbiter and guide in the therapeutic process.*(pp. 1–6)

The music therapist should not conduct sessions in psychodrama without the proper training. However, the music therapist can utilize some of the dramatic techniques of psychodrama within the music therapy session—even more so with the assistance of someone who has been trained in psychodramatic techniques.

For those who have training in both music therapy and psychodrama, there is a new technique developed by Joseph Moreno, R.M.T., which combines the two modalities into what he calls "musical psychodrama." A musical improvisatory ensemble is the added tool in the process. Its function is to reinforce and bring out the feelings of the protagonist. In a paper and demonstration on musical psychodrama which Moreno presented at the Canadian Association for Music Therapy con-

*From Psychodrama and Group Psychotherapy Monograph, No. 41, Beacon House, Inc., Beacon, N.Y., 1966, and Group Psychotherapy Vol. XVIII, 1965, J. L. Moreno, M.D., Editor, Beacon House Inc., Beacon, N.Y., Publisher.

ference in Toronto, Ontario, May 10–12, 1979, he outlined general guidelines for clinical applications; gave suggestions on instrumentation, improvisation, cuing techniques, and stage placement; discussed clinical experiences and dream exploration; and emphasized the importance and commonality of the elements shared by the two therapies, such as the focus on the "here and now" and spontaneity, the interaction and reinforcement of a group setting, and the use of sound and improvisation.

Although the possibilities of musical psychodrama are exciting, it should not be attempted by the untrained music therapist or lay person. However, there are other ways in which music therapy and drama can be successfully employed together. This chapter presents some of the possibilities for incorporating drama into music therapy sessions in the following activities: roles (Wolfe et al., 1975); dramatic improvisation and music (Paynter & Aston, 1970); background music (no specific reference); and body communication (former colleague, 1975).

ROLES

Purpose of the Activity

To promote socialization via verbal interaction and cooperation in a group setting.

To encourage group members to examine roles which they have assumed in their own lives, as well as any changes which they have made, or would like to make, in these roles.

To encourage concentration and participation.

To provide enjoyment.

Procedure for Action

The group is instructed to list the roles and their responsibilities as given in the song "Tradition" from the musical "Fiddler on the Roof." Following this, each group member compiles another list of roles and their responsibilities, but of those assumed during their lives. This list is put together according to three categories: past roles, present roles, and future roles. Then each person chooses a song to describe a role on this list, plays it, and explains which role it is and why the song was chosen to depict this role. This role and the other roles on the list are discussed by the group. Many avenues of discussion are possible, such as how the roles in all three categories may overlap; how some roles, by necessity, change throughout life; how the same role can be handled differently by each person; how to make positive changes in a present role for the future.

When a group is to large too deal with each individual's roles, subgroups may be formed. Members of each subgroup discuss their lists of individual roles among themselves and, as a group, choose a record which they feel describes one role they all have in common. Further discussion of the record and the role it depicts may be kept within each subgroup or carried on throughout the whole, larger group.

Rules Governing Action

There are no specific rules, but the group may decide on some for a particular session.

Number of Required Participants

One or more.

Roles of Participants

Each person should try to think of as many roles assumed and should participate as much as possible in discussing them.

Results or Payoff

The opportunity to examine the roles assumed in one's life and any possible positive changes that can be made for the future.

Abilities and Skills Required for Action

Cognitive—the abilities to recall and evaluate.
Sensory-motor—the physical abilities to write and communicate verbally.
Affective—the ability to relate to one's feelings as well as those of others.

Interaction Patterns

Intra-individual, aggregate, intra-group.

Physical Setting and Environmental Requirements

Any setting that is comfortable and available for meeting.

Required Equipment

A record player and records, possibly a piano, and paper and pencils.

DRAMATIC IMPROVISATION AND MUSIC

Purpose of the Activity

To allow participants to become more aware of and to make use of the sound and space in their environment.
To promote socialization via group interaction and cooperation.

To encourage concentration and on-task behavior.
To promote imagination and creativity.
To provide a satisfying and positive experience.
To provide enjoyment.

Procedure for Action

Have the group members divide themselves into smaller subgroups, allotting each a work space at a reasonable distance from other subgroups. Allow each of these subgroups to look at and handle some object which the therapist has chosen as a stimulus to the imagination. The groups are then instructed that they will be given a few minutes to make up a story using the object as their starting point.

At the end of the allotted time, whether the stories are completed or not, have an appointed spokesman from each subgroup relate their story. On hearing each story, try to get the subgroups to give some indication of whether they feel that music would aid them in what they are trying to say dramatically: Would music be needed all the time? If not, which parts would especially benefit from the addition of some background music (not to be confused with sound effects)?

It might be helpful to use one subgroup as an example, discussing the possibilities of where and how to use music appropriately. The therapist may offer suggestions but should try to encourage the groups to make their own decisions on the actual nature of the music. Each group should be encouraged to make some kind of music, no matter how simple, and each group should be given the opportunity to perform its story. After all the performances, encourage discussion to compare versions.

Rules Governing Action

Only the time limits set by the therapist.

Number of Required Participants

Three or more.

Roles of Participants

To play an active part in the preparation and actual performance of a story, as well as in the discussions.

Results or Payoff

The opportunity to express oneself in a nonthreatening situation and to enjoy it.

Abilities and Skills Required for Action

Cognitive—imagination and creativity.
Sensory-motor—the ability to act out the story and/or to provide the music.
Affective—the ability to work well with others.

Interaction Patterns

Intra-individual, aggregate, intra-group.

Physical Setting and Environmental Requirements

A large enough area for the groups to work in.

Required Equipment

An assortment of instruments and recordings, a record player, and the stimulus object.

BACKGROUND MUSIC

Purpose of This Activity

To help participants become more aware of the sounds in their environment.

To encourage concentration and on-task behavior.

To promote listening and interpretive skills.

To promote socialization via verbal interaction and cooperation in a group setting.

To provide enjoyment.

Procedure for Action

Arrange to have the group see a film or television play which has had music specially composed for it. Instruct the group to pay special attention to the music and note any especially effective episodes. The following questions may be suggested to the group before viewing the film as guidelines on what to look for: What types of sounds are used for the especially effective episodes (if any at all), and how do they relate to the dramatic situations? Is music used a lot? Are any particular emotions conveyed by the use of music or the lack of it? If so, can these emotions be classified (happiness, elation, sadness, despair, fear, a sense of the sinister)? Did the texture of the music (whether it was simple or complex) make a difference? What other characteristics of music seemed to have an effect on the viewer's reactions? It may also be helpful to study a play from the script and to listen to the music written specifically for that play (for example, Ibsen's "Peer Gynt" with Grieg's incidental music, Shakespeare's "A Midsummer Night's Dream" with Mendelssohn's incidental music).

A variation of this procedure is to play a recording of any

type (but preferably without words) as background music for a play on television with the sound on the TV turned down. This really accentuates the role music plays as background to a performance. Discussion is encouraged.

Rules Governing Action

None.

Number of Required Participants

One or more.

Roles of Participants

To listen attentively and take part in the discussion on how music in the background of a performance affects the reactions of its viewers.

Results or Payoff

Simply the enjoyment which may result from becoming more aware of one's environment.

Abilities and Skills Required for Action

Cognitive—listening and interpretive skills.
Sensory-motor—the ability to communicate.
Affective—the ability to relate to one's feelings as well as to those of others.

Interaction Patterns

Intra-individual, aggregate, intra-group.

Physical Setting and Environmental Requirements

Wherever a film or television play may be viewed and later discussed.

Required Equipment

Projector and film or television, play scripts and their corresponding recordings, and a record player.

BODY COMMUNICATION

Purpose of the Activity

To help participants become aware of their body communication of reactions and attitudes.

To encourage group members to examine goals in life and standards of character they hope to obtain.

To gain the confidence to express and share one's opinions and emotions to others more freely.

To promote socialization via group interaction and cooperation.

To provide a positive experience.

Procedure for Action

Have the group members express their reactions to a variety of feelings, such as tension, relaxation, anger, joy, heat, cold, physical pain, emotional pain, pleasure, courage, fear, happiness, sadness, sexiness, innocence, guilt, love, hate, excitement, exhaustion, surprise, expectation, disappointment, satisfaction, curiousity, apathy, understanding, and confusion—in their feet and legs, hips and waist, chest and shoulders, hands and arms, and neck and head, in each of these parts separately or in combinations or all together with their whole bodies, but with no facial expressions. Next have the group express their reactions to a variety of feelings (the same as before or others) via facial expressions and the use of a rhythm instrument, but with no body expression. (Feelings may be mixed in both instances).

After these exercises, say to the group, "Pretend you are a statue of youself: How would you stand?" Each group member is to choose music which he or she feels is self-representative. The group then guesses from the music how this person would stand. After some guesses are made (correct or not), the group member shows how he or she would stand as a statue, explains why he or she would stand in this way and how the music relates to the stance.

After each group member has shown a stand, discussion should be encouraged with questions like these: What facial expressions do you want people to know you for and why? What character are you portraying in your pose, and are you like that now or is it your goal to achieve such a character?

Can you change to be as you want to be, and if you can, what steps or actions can you take to achieve such a goal? What do you especially not want people to know you as and why? If people misjudge you for what you are, how can you show them what you really are?

Rules Governing Action

None.

Number of Required Participants

Two or more.

Roles of Participants

Each person should try to express reactions to as many different types of feelings as possible, should find a stand and music that represents it, and should actively participate in the discussion.

Results or Payoff

The opportunity to examine one's body communication, standards of character, goals in life, and any possible changes that can be made for the future.

Abilities and Skills Required for Action

Cognitive—the abilities to express and evaluate.

Sensory-motor—the ability to express reactions to a variety of feelings in all parts of the body, and to communicate.

Affective—the ability to relate to others as well as to oneself.

Interaction Patterns

Intra-individual, aggregate, intra-group.

Physical Setting and Environmental Requirements

Any setting that is comfortable and available for meeting.

Required Equipment

A variety of musical recordings and a record player, and an assortment of rhythm instruments.

Chapter 12

ORFF AND KODÁLY

Carl Orff, a contemporary Bavarian composer-conductor-educator, was responsible for the development of *Schulwerk* (German for *schoolwork*) in Munich, Germany. *Schulwerk* is the use of elemental music (one's own contribution using music, rhythm, movement, voice, speech and silence) in learning through discovery. Orff believed that feeling precedes intellectual understanding. With this in mind, he evolved an approach to music education that starts with the most basic element of music, rhythm. He felt that a child would be best encouraged, and best equipped, to explore music through the rhythm of the child's speech and movement. (These concepts reflect the influence of another contemporary composer-educator-innovator, Emile Jacques-Dàlcroze, whose work is discussed in the following chapter.)

Schulwerk consists of four phases: the germ idea, development, exploration, and closure. Combining experience, learning, and success in co-composership, the most commonly used forms in *Schulwerk* can be simple or complex: rondos, ostinati, inventions, call-responses, speech patterns, pentatonic scales, chants, proverbs, rhymes, and games. The group process of *Schulwerk* integrates music, movement, mime, language, poetry, art, and creative dramatics.

Easy, successful experiences are made possible in the development of communication skills, sensorimotor skills, social skills, self-help skills, behavior control, modeling, realization of self-worth, cause and effect, exploration of feelings and affect, and learning basic concepts. Each participant contributes to this process (regardless of the level of ability, this contribution is always accepted) and is encouraged to further develop his ideas. Since 1950 Orff and his collaborators have produced a variety of Orff-*Schulwerk* instruments, books, records, films, and other material to be used as resources.

Zoltán Kodály, a contemporary Hungarian composer-conductor-educator, was responsible for the development of a sequential system of sight singing which leads to the understanding of musical notation. Although his concepts have not yet been fully developed or standardized for use, Kodály's approach to rhythmic counting and his use of hand signals have been successful in aiding the development of inner hearing and feeling.

Kodály believed that when a child has had a significant amount of experience in responding to rhythm, the child is ready to see what he has experienced, to count it rhythmically, and to notate it. Kodály applied this idea to pitch as well. From the basic system of hand signals developed by the Englishman John Curwen in 1870, Kodály developed a method that enables a child to "see" the general height (or depth) of the sound the child hears.

Although Orff and Kodály agreed on many of the aspects of the rhythmic and melodic development of the child, their approaches vary: Kodály believed that specific music reading skills should be developed early in a child's growth, whereas Orff was not concerned with music reading. As a result, the two approaches complement one another and may be successfully combined.

Many of the concepts that make these two methods particularly effective in music education are concepts that are used in music therapy. The main concern of both men was that every child should be able to enjoy and participate in music. Gaston (1968) stated that "all mankind has need for aesthetic expression and experience" (p. 21). Both men carefully considered the structure of music and its presentation. Gaston stated that "music is structured reality" (p. 24). Easy successful experiences are made available in both approaches. Gaston also held that "music is a source of gratification" (p. 26). Both methods make use of the various elements and forms of music to communicate. Gaston believed that "music" is communication" (p. 23) and "music is derived from the tender emotions" (p. 24). The use of the pentatonic scale in both methods is universal. A variety of chants, proverbs and rhymes employed by both methods are universal as well—they need only be translated from one language to another. Gaston stated that "the cultural matrix determines the mode of expression" (p. 22). And both methods are primarily employed in group situations. Finally, Gaston wrote that "the potency of music is greatest in the group" (p. 27). In view of these related concepts, the following activities are presented in this chapter: body echoes (Grenoble, 1977); Orff rondos (Bitcon, 1976); solfège and rhythm (Wheeler & Raebeck, 1972); Orff and Kodály combined (Wheeler & Raebeck, 1972).

BODY ECHOES

Purpose of the Activity

To promote perceptual-motor coordination.

To enable group members to develop a sense of rhythmic awareness.

To encourage the utilization of different body parts.

To enable group members to develop body orientation.

To provide a means of nonverbal communication.

To promote socialization via group interaction and cooperation.

To provide less verbal group members with an activity in which they may participate more fully.

To provide enjoyment.

Procedure for Action

Everyone is seated in a circle. The therapist says, "Do as I do after me," in slow, straight quarter-note rhythm, followed by a simple body rhythm such as clapping his hands in four straight quarter notes. Other rhythmic movements should be used as well, such as slapping the thighs, snapping the fingers, stamping the feet. Depending on the skill of the group, the rhythms can be made more complex, different parts of the body can be combined, everyone can take turns being the leader, rhythm instruments can be used with or without music, or body echoes (see last page of activity) can be done as part of a song.

Rules Governing Action

There are no specific rules, but the group may decide on some for a particular session.

Number of Required Participants

A minimum of two, no stated maximum.

Roles of Participants

To repeat the rhythms together with the rest of the group, and possibly to initiate some for the group to follow.

Results or Payoff

The simple enjoyment of taking part in such an activity.

Abilities and Skills Required for Action

Cognitive—rhythmic and perceptual awareness and creativity.

Sensory-motor—perceptual-motor coordination of all body parts.

Affective—the ability to work well with others rhythmically.

Interaction Patterns

Intra-individual, aggregate, intra-group.

Physical Setting and Environmental Requirements

Any setting that is comfortable and available for meeting.

Required Equipment

Only the participants are actually necessary, but rhythm instruments and other musical accompaniment may be added.

ORFF RONDOS

Purpose of the Activity

To promote socialization via group interaction and cooperation.

To enable group members to develop a sense of rhythmic awareness.

To promote perceptual-motor coordination.

To provide a means of nonverbal communication.

To encourage the utilization of imagination and creativity.

To provide less verbal group members with an activity in which they may participate more fully.

I'm Gonna Sing

Spiritual (Adapted)

I'm gon-na sing when the spi-rit says sing.
I'm gon-na clap when the spi-rit says clap.
I'm gon-na snap when the spi-rit says snap.
I'm gon-na pat when the spi-rit says pat.
I'm gon-na stamp when the spi-rit says stamp.

I'm gon-na sing when the spi-rit says sing.
I'm gon-na clap when the spi-rit says clap.
I'm gon-na snap when the spi-rit says snap.
I'm gon-na pat when the spi-rit says pat.
I'm gon-na stamp when the spi-rit says stamp.

I'm gon-na sing when the spi-rit says sing.
I'm gon-na clap when the spi-rit says clap.
I'm gon-na snap when the spi-rit says snap.
I'm gon-na pat when the spi-rit says pat.
I'm gon-na stamp when the spi-rit says stamp.

O-bey the word of the Lord. (Do body echo)
O-bey the word of the Lord. (Do body echo)
O-bey the word of the Lord. (Do body echo)
O-bey the word of the Lord. (Do body echo)
O-bey the word of the Lord. (Do body echo)

To encourage concentration and on-task behavior.

To make possible an easy successful experience in an enjoyable way.

Procedure for Action

Like communication in songs, chants, or rhythms, Orff-*Schulwerk* is partially nonverbal; that is, the Orff method emphasizes the rhythm in speech and body movement. Using the failure-proof pentatonic scale on high-quality percussion (Orff) instruments, group members enhance their creative faculties by creating their own music. The rondo form is one of the most popular of the many forms used in the original Orff context. It provides for repetition of the subject (A) and allows each group member to respond individually (response B, response C, response D, and so on), in the following pattern: A:B:A:C:A:D:A. Orff rondos are usually sing-song chants accompanied by body rhythms (presented at the end of this activity). However, Orff rondos may also be arranged to be played on Orff Instruments. Activities (rondos) can be constructed to meet almost any goal.

Rules Governing Action

Only those set by the group for a particular session.

Number of Required Participants

One or more.

Roles of Participants

To perform the rondos as creatively as possible.

Results or Payoff

Simply the enjoyment of taking part in such an activity.

Abilities and Skills Required for Action

Cognitive—auditory-visual perception, a sense of rhythm, imagination, and creativity.

Sensory-motor—perceptual-motor coordination.

Affective—the ability to work well with others.

Interaction Patterns

Intra-individual, aggregate, intra-group.

Physical Setting and Environmental Requirements

Any setting that is comfortable and available for meeting.

Required Equipment

Orff instruments.

Examples of Orff Rondos (with movements)

Names, names, names are fine;
You tell me yours and I'll tell you mine.
(Name accompanied by body rhythm)

Names have music just like song;
Play your name and pass it along.
(Rhythm of name is played on a rhythm instrument)

Sometimes I'm happy, sometimes I'm sad;
Sometimes I'm all worn out, sometimes I'm mad.
How do you feel? (Answer accompanied by body rhythm)

Um, um, good, um, um, good,
Tell us what you think is um, um, good.
(Answer accompanied by the playing of its rhythm)

Music, music, in the air;
Make some music a friend can share.
(A musical phrase is composed on the pentatonic scale)

Arms, legs, hands, feet;
Pick one out and make a beat.
(A rhythmic pattern is produced by one of these body parts)

Exercise, exercise, let's do some exercise;
Hands over head, fingers on your toes;
Show us how *your* exercise goes.
(A movement pattern is produced by one or more body parts)

Make your voice high, make your voice low;
Make your voice go where you want it to go.
(Voice activity—self-explanatory)

I'm a person and so are you;
Jump into the circle and show us what you do.
(Activity on uniqueness—self-explanatory)

Solfège and Rhythm

Purpose of the Activity

To enable group members to develop inner hearing and a feeling for rhythm and pitch.

To promote perceptual motor-coordination.

To encourage concentration and on-task behavior.

To promote socialization via group interaction and cooperation.

To provide less verbal group members with an activity in which they may participate more fully.

To make possible an easy successful experience in an enjoyable way.

Procedure for Action

The Kodály method emphasizes the use of vocal music, with a focus on relative solmization and its relation to visual symbolization. In simple terms, there is a corresponding hand signal for each syllable used in the solfège. Considerable time is spent in learning intervals and carefully listening to their correct production. Via this system, the group can learn to sing with very good intonation, can learn to read notation, and can understand concepts of harmony in a relatively short time.

Rhythm is first taught through movement; then the concepts are related to certain syllables: "ta" represents a quarter note, "te" an eighth note, "ti-ri" sixteenth notes, and so on. Physical movement is strongly encouraged. Through these two systems, songs can be learned easily and quickly by rote. Rhythmic ostinati, canons, and other variations may be used to give each group member the chance to participate individually and to provide some challenge and interest.

Rules Governing Action

To follow the signals of the leader.

Number of Required Participants

One or more.

Roles of Participants

To match the given hand signals with the correct pitches; to reproduce rhythmic patterns correctly; and to vocalize the appropriate syllables in the appropriate places.

Results or payoff

Development of singing and rhythmic abilities, and simultaneous enjoyment of the process.

Abilities and Skills Required for Action

Cognitive—rhythmic and pitch perception.
Sensory-motor—perceptual-motor coordination.
Affective—the ability to work well with others.

Interaction Patterns

Intra-individual, aggregate, intra-group.

Physical Setting and Environmental Requirements

Any setting that is comfortable and available for meeting.

Required Equipment

A blackboard and chalk, a pitch pipe, and, possibly, a rhythm box of a variety of rhythms.

Kodály/Dàlcroze (see Chapter 8)

Chart of Rhythmic Counting and Clapping

Quarter notes (♩)

Notation:	│	│	│	│
Count:	Beat	beat	beat	beat
Clap:	Clap	clap	clap	clap

Eighth notes (♪)

Notation:	⌐¬	⌐¬	⌐¬	⌐¬
Count:	Two 8ths	two 8ths	two 8ths	two 8ths
Clap:	Clap clap	clap clap	clap clap	clap clap

Half notes (♩)

Notation:	♩		♩	
Count:	Half	note	Half	note
Clap:	Clap	(Move one hand upward for length of note)	Clap	(Move one hand upward for length of note)

Dotted half notes (♩·)

Notation:	♩.			♩.		
Count:	Half	note	dot	Half	note	dot
Clap:	Clap	(Move one hand upward to imaginary dot in air)	(Move one hand upward)	Clap	(Move one hand upward to imaginary dot in air)	(Move one hand upward)

Whole notes (o)

Notation:	o			
Count:	Great	big	whole	note
Clap:	Clap	(Move one hand upward for length of note)		

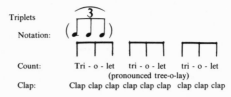

Triplets

Notation:

Count: Tri - o - let   tri - o - let   tri - o - let
                (pronounced tree-o-lay)

Clap: Clap clap clap clap clap clap   clap clap clap

Sixteenth notes

Notation:

Count: Boom ah chick ah Boom ah chick ah

Clap: Clap clap clap clap   clap clap clap clap

Rests   (𝄽 or 𝄾 or 𝄿)

Notation: 𝄾   (or one of above)

Count: Rest (spoken)

Clap: No clapping. Move hands forward, palms up;
                or tap fingers of left hand left shoulder
                and simultaneously, fingers of right hand on
                right shoulder; or bring index finger to lips.

Combinations of eighth and sixteenth notes

Notation:

Count: Boom   chick   ah   Boom   ah   chick
            (or 8th)   (or 8th)

Clap: Clap   clap   clap   clap   clap   clap

Ties

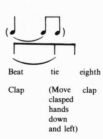

Notation:

Count: Beat   tie   eighth

Clap: Clap   (Move   clap
                  clasped
                  hands
                  down
                  and left)

Dotted quarter and eighth note (♩. ♪)

	Notation:			
		|	•	⅄
	Count:	Beat	dot	dot
	Clap:	Clap	(move one hand to imaginary dot in air)	clap

Dotted eighth and sixteenth note (♪. ♪)

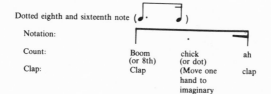

	Notation:			
	Count:	Boom (or 8th)	chick (or dot)	ah
	Clap:	Clap	(Move one hand to imaginary dot in air)	clap

Syncopation a. (♪ ♩ ♪)   (♪ ♩ ♪)

	Notation:							
		⅄	|	⅄				
	Count:	Syn - co - pah			Syn - co - pah			
	Clap:	Clap	clap (On second half of **note,** move one hand up for length of note)	clap	Clap	clap (On second half of note, move one hand up for length of note)	clap	

b. (♪ ♩.)   (♪ ♪.)

	Notation:						
		⅄	|	•	⅄	⅄ •
	Count:	Syn - co-(*Think* pah) Syn - co-(*Think* pah)				
	Clap:	Clap clap (Move one hand to imaginary dot in air)		Clap clap (move one hand to imaginary dot in air)		

193

Kodály Chart of Hand Signals

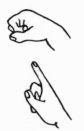 DO¹ or 1¹ (arm's length above head)

TI or 7

 LA or 6

 SO or 5 (even with eyes)

FA or 4 (shoulder level)

 MI or 3 (even with chest)

 RE or 2

 DO or 1 (waist level)

Note: In any scale the first seven tones are noted with syllables only. Tones from high Do and up are indicated with a "1" above each syllable; tones below low Do are indicated with a "1" below the syllable, for lower octave.

ORFF AND KODÁLY COMBINED*

Purpose of the Activity

To enable group members to develop inner hearing and a feeling for rhythm and pitch.

To promote perceptual-motor coordination.

To encourage concentration and on-task behavior.

To encourage creativity.

To promote socialization via group interaction and cooperation.

To provide less verbal group members with an activity in which they may participate more fully.

To make possible an easy successful experience in an enjoyable way.

Procedure for Action

Have the group do some echo movement, ending with the following pattern:

Left shoulder
Right shoulder
Clap
Patschen

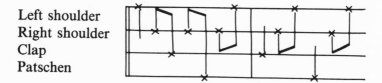

(Note: The left hand taps the right shoulder, and the right hand taps the left shoulder.) Tell the group to continue doing this pattern as the therapist sings "Swing Low, Sweet Chariot." The song is begun with the chorus, on the last beat of the second measure, and the group should be encouraged to sing along. After the song is completed, notate it on the blackboard in

*This activity is included by permission of Lawrence Wheeler and Lois Raebeck, from *Orff and Kodály Adapted for the Elementary School,* second edition. Wm. C. Brown Company, Publishers © 1972, 1977.

whole notes, using the correct number of notes in each measure. If possible, have group members notate the song melodically. Then ask the group if they can notate the song rhythmically.

First, they are to listen to the therapist chant and clap the first phrase and then echo it. The first phrase is chanted and clapped again by the therapist, but using number notation with it, and then the group echoes it again. A volunteer is then asked to notate the first phrase rhythmically, with help where necessary. (It may be necessary to review syncopation for the second measure.) This is continued until the entire song is notated rhythmically. Then have the group clap and chant the number notation of the song all the way through. The entire song is sung by the whole group again, with them accompanying themselves with the rhythmic movement practiced earlier. The rhythmic movement is begun first; after one measure and three beats, the group is signalled to begin singing the chorus.

This procedure may be expanded on in the following ways: An ostinato accompaniment may be added to the final production; this song may be combined with a partner song, and both songs may be sung simultaneously; individual group members may sing solos on the verses; and group members may create rhythmic interpretations of the chorus or verses.

Rules Governing Action

To follow the signals of the leader.

Number of Required Participants

One or more.

Roles of Participants

To make the echo movements, sing the song, notate the song melodically and rhythmically, clap and chant the number notation of the song, combine the rhythmic movement with singing the song, sing a partner song against this song, create rhythmic interpretations of the song, and so on.

Results or Payoff

Development of singing and rhythmic abilities, and simultaneous enjoyment of the process.

Abilities and Skills Required for Action

Cognitive—rhythmic and pitch perception.
Sensory-motor—perceptual-motor coordination.
Affective—the ability to work with others.

Interaction Patterns

Intra-individual, aggregate, intra-group.

Physical Setting and Environmental Requirements

Any setting that is comfortable and available for meeting.

Required Equipment

A blackboard and chalk, a pitch pipe and instruments.

Chapter 13

EURHYTHMICS

Eurhythmics, a definite and carefully worked-out system of musical training through physical movement, was developed between 1900 and 1912 by Emile Jacques-Dàlcroze. During his years as professor of solfège at the Geneva Conservatoire, Jacques-Dàlcroze found the traditional methods of musical training to be unsatisfactory. He felt that the body needed to be developed with the mind at an early age. He soon came to realize that the musical element of primary appeal to children is rhythm, that the natural response to rhythm is physical, and that the body should be the child's "first instrument" through which to reflect and interpret the movement and nuances in music.

Eurhythmics has been developed in many ways by many people in many parts of the world since its birth, but there are certain intrinsic characteristics in every good Dàlcroze lesson: the essential pleasure of rhythmic movement and the confidence that it gives; the abilities to hear, comprehend, and interpret music in movement; and the invitations to pupils to improvise and develop their own ideas freely.

Music is vital to and inseparable from Dàlcroze's method of eurhythmics. In addition to its educational value, Jacques-Dàlcroze recognized the power of music as a therapeutic agent. All exercises in eurhythmics deal with the promotion of attention, concentration, memory; perception of space and perception of the body; contact with others, the sense of responsibility, and social interaction; balance, coordination of movement, and independence of movements; imagination, sensitivity, originality, and creativity; play and symbolic expression; and relaxation.

In view of these therapeutic goals and the extent to which eurhythmics has been used successfully in therapy, the following exercises are presented: jumping over the gate (Findlay, 1971); movement canon (Findlay, 1971); gavotte II (Findlay, 1971); and, machines (former colleague, 1976).*

Jumping Over the Gate

Purpose of the Activity

To enable group members to develop a sense of rhythm throughout the body.

To encourage the utilization of different body parts.

To promote socialization via group interaction and cooperation.

To enable group members to develop rhythmic-motor coordination.

To provide an enjoyable experience.

Procedure for Action

Arrange the group members in sets of threes: *A, B, C.* *A*s and *B*s are paired off and kneel and hold hands to represent the gate, while *C*s stand some distance behind them. The *C*s

---

*Activities are included by permission of Elsa Findlay from *Rhythm and Movement:* Application of Dàlcroze Eurhythmics. Evanston, Illinois: Summy-Birchard Company, 1971.

and jump over their gates, kneel, and then stand to this rhythm and chant:

All As and Bs remain kneeling, while Cs jump over a different gate each time.

For able groups, the game can become more complicated as As and Bs kneel, stand, run forward six steps and kneel to this rhythm and movement sequence and chant:

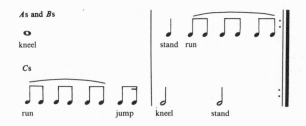

Meanwhile, Cs standing at some distance behind As and Bs, run forward six steps, jump over the gates, kneel and stand, and are then ready to begin their sequence all over again. This rhythm and movement sequence, with chant, is the same as the initial one. The two movements and rhythms, with chants, of both As and Bs, and Cs together are:

As and Bs
kneel   stand run

Cs
run   jump kneel   stand

Rules Governing Action

To follow the movement sequence of the exercise.

Number of Required Participants

Three or more.

Roles of Participants

To follow the moves of whatever letter they are assigned —*A, B,* or *C*—in the correct rhythms and with the chants.

Results or Payoff

Simply the fun of the game.

Abilities and Skills Required for Action

Cognitive—a sense of rhythm and recall of movements. Sensory-motor—the ability to run, jump, kneel, and stand. Affective—the ability to work well with others.

Interaction Patterns

Intra-individual, aggregate, intra-group.

Physical Setting and Environmental Requirements

A large, open floor area.

Required Equipment

Nothing is actually needed except the people themselves, but some musical accompaniment may be used.

MOVEMENT CANON

Purpose of the Activity

To enable group members to develop a sense of rhythm throughout the body.

To promote listening and concentration skills.

To encourage the utilization of different body parts.

To help group members develop rhythmic-motor coordination.

To promote socialization via group interaction and cooperation.

To provide an enjoyable experience.

Procedure for Action

Group members are instructed to sit on their feet with their hands touching the floor, pretending to play the piano: Their left hands are to interpret what the therapist plays in the bass, while their right hands interpret the treble. The rhythms should be simple and very clearly defined. At command, the group steps the following rhythmic patterns: ♫ ♫ ♫ ♫ (4/4); ♫ ♫ ♫ (3/4); ♫ ♫ (2/4). (Note that the last example is the most difficult.)

When the movements to these patterns have been mastered, divide the group into three circles, each one representing a rhythmic pattern. The circles have to listen to the rhythms played by the therapist and interpret which of the three it is; then the circle that represents that rhythm is to step it out.

This is an interrupted canon, and may be improvised on. The therapist improvises a simple measure in 4/4 rhythm and then rests for one measure. During this measure of silence, the group claps and/or steps the rhythmic pattern that was just played; then they rest for a measure, while the therapist plays another rhythmic pattern. This is continued in the following manner:

When the group feels comfortable doing interrupted canons, they may try well-known rounds such as "Frère Jacques."

First the rhythms should be clapped, then stepped, then written on a blackboard by the group members. The group is then divided into four files and interprets the round in movement. (They should be encouraged to sing as they move).

To give the group a better concept of the form of a round, mark off four areas on the floor, one for each phrase of "Frère Jacques," to form a square. Place four group members, *A, B, C, D,* at the first mark. *A* steps from the first mark to the second mark for the first phrase of the song, steps to the third space for the second phrase, and so on until the first mark is reached again and the song is ended. *B* begins the first phrase as *A* moves from the second to third marks. *C* begins the first phrase as *B* moves from the second to third marks. *D* begins the first phrase as *C* moves from the second to third marks, and so on. In this manner, *B, C,* and *D* are imitating *A*s rhythms and directions.

The group is now ready for a movement canon. Arranged in one large circle, group members are numbered off in threes. In nine counts they walk toward the center of the circle, slowly lifting their arms; and in nine counts they walk backwards to their original positions, slowly lowering their arms. This forward-and-backward movement describes a crescendo and decrescendo.

Once the whole group feels comfortable with this movement, have only the No. 1s begin walking to the center and back. No. 2s begin their forward movement on the fourth count of the No. 1s, but the No. 2s count it as their first count. No. 3s begin their forward movement on the seventh count of the No. 1s, but the No. 3s count it as their first count. Each number completes the full nine-count cycle and then begins again.

This whole movement represents a canon in nine counts and must be done with a certain amount of tension as each numbered group reaches its climax. To add to the expression, each numbered group may carry a different colored scarf, for example red scarves for No. 1s, yellow for No. 2s, and green for No. 3s.

Rules Governing Action

To follow the movement sequence of the exercise.

Number of Required Participants

Three or more.

Roles of Participants

To follow the moves as a group, or in whatever smaller group each is assigned to (circles, letters, or numbers), in the correct rhythms. When songs are used, the group should be encouraged to sing along as well.

Results or Payoff

Simply the fun of such an activity.

Abilities and Skills Required for Action

Cognitive—a sense of rhythm, auditory perception, concentration, and recall.
Sensory-motor—the ability to clap and step in time.
Affective—the ability to work well with others.

Interaction Patterns

Intra-individual, aggregate, intra-group.

Physical Setting and Environmental Requirements

A large, open floor area.

Required Equipment

Nothing is actually necessary except the people themselves, but musical accompaniment may be helpful.

GAVOTTE II

Purpose of the Activity

To help group members develop a sense of rhythm throughout the body.
To promote listening and concentration skills.
To encourage the utilization of different body parts.
To help group members develop rhythmic-motor coordination.
To promote socialization via group interaction and cooperation.
To provide an enjoyable experience.

Procedure for Action

The group must have had experience in working with rhythmic patterns, phrases, and simple forms before attempting this activity on interpretation through movement. There is an abundance of suitable music that may be interpreted in simple space and movement patterns, but there must be an understanding of the form and a respect for the music used. Therefore the therapist must take great care in choosing the music to be used for a specific group. Some groups may even be able to compose their own music.

J. S. Bach's "Gavotte II" from his "English Suite No. 6" is an example of a piece in ABA form which may be interpreted in the following way.

Section A. Half the group stands in the center of the room holding hands. As the music begins, they step the rhythmic pattern, moving lightly on their toes clockwise, beginning with their left feet on the anacrusis. To accommodate longer held notes, they lift their right legs slightly on the dot of the dotted quarter note and stop on the half note. This movement pattern is repeated twice more until they reach the eighth notes and the end of this section. Then the whole section is repeated counter-clockwise. When Section *A* has been completed, they stand quietly in the center of the room, side by side.

Section B. The other half of the group now moves in a circle counter-clockwise around the center group. Their movement is the same as that of the *A* group, except that they hold their arms lightly extended at shoulder level. At the end of Section *B,* they join the *A* group to form one large circle, *A*s and *B*s alternating.

Second section A. The last section is done by both the *A*s and *B*s in this large circle. (The repeat may also be done by everyone together, or they may split up into the two groups again). At the end of the piece, the *A*s stand on tiptoes while the *B*s kneel beside them, everyone continuing to hold hands.

Rules Governing Action

To follow the movement sequence of the exercise.

Number of Required Participants

Six or more.

Roles of Participants

To follow the rhythmic-movement patterns correctly.

Results or Payoff

Simply the fun of such an activity.

Abilities and Skills Required for Action

Cognitive—a sense of rhythm, auditory perception, concentration, and recall.

Sensory-motor—the ability to move body parts in time.

Affective—the ability to work well with others.

Interaction Patterns

Intra-individual, aggregate, intra-group.

Physical Setting and Environmental Requirements

A large, open floor area.

Required Equipment

The music that is to be interpreted and the means by which it is to be played (such as a record player or piano).

Gavotte I d. C.

MACHINES

Purpose of the Activity

To encourage self-expression.

To stimulate imagination and creativity.

To encourage the utilization of different body parts.

To provide a means for nonverbal communication.

To promote socialization via group interaction and cooperation.

To help group members become more aware of one's environment.

To provide an enjoyable experience.

Procedure for Action

First discuss the concepts of the "whole determing the parts" or the "whole being the sum of its parts". Relate this to the idea of a working, functioning human being in relation to his or her environment, and to how everything that is alive has a rhythm or beat that can be used as a measure of its ability to function.

Either suggest to one member of the group or have that member think of a certain machine that is made of many parts and which, when all are working in fairly good condition, will produce an effectively operating machine. Have that person become or express a single part of that machine through the rhythmic use of his body. As soon as someone else in the group has some idea of what type of machine is being acted out, he also becomes a "part." This continues until every member of the group becomes a "part of the whole." For those who have no idea what type of machine is being acted out, they should make up new parts possibly to produce a new machine.

Music that can be related to a certain type of machine may be used to start the process, or music may be used just as background music. All should be encouraged to participate, and after the machine is completed, the "parts" should try to discover how they are working in relation to one another. Rhythm instruments may be used to suggest sounds of machines.

Do not stay on one machine too long, but move on to a new idea, asking someone else to be the first part. Discussion may be initiated at the end of the whole activity, once again to talk about the effects of working together and related topics.

Rules Governing Action

The only clues on what machine is being simulated should come from the "body rhythms" of the "parts"—there should be no talking, though sounds may be used to act out the parts. A time limit and other strictures may be decided on by the group once they understand the activity.

Number of Required Participants

A minimum of five; no maximum.

Roles of Participants

To guess what machines are acted out, to assume a part, to become aware of the relationship of the parts working together, and possibly to discuss it.

Results or Payoff

The fun of being able to guess the machines being acted out and then to become a part of those machines.

Abilities and Skills Required for Action

Cognitive—perceptual awareness, self-expression, imagination, and creativity.

Sensory-motor—the ability to communicate with parts of one's body.

Affective—the ability to communicate with others nonverbally.

Interaction Patterns

Intra-individual, aggregate, intra-group.

Physical Setting and Environmental Requirements

A large floor area.

Required Equipment

A record player and records, tape recorder and tapes, and/or some instruments.

Chapter 14

GUIDED IMAGERY

Man has been aware for some time that listening to music is one of the pathways leading to the deepening and expanding of non-ordinary levels of human consciousness. However, there was no procedure that used music in this way with any predictable results, until Helen L. Bonny and Dr. Louis Savary successfully devised such techniques, creating the field of "guided imagery." And in the pursuit of furthering the field of guided imagery, Bonny founded the Institute for Consciousness and Music in Baltimore, Maryland.

Some of the general purposes of the Institute are:

1. To engage in research, writing, training, and education leading to the development and expansion of the areas and depth of human consciousness through music listening (guided imagery).
2. To investigate the science of music to develop and facilitate non-drug-induced "altered states of consciousness" in order to expand awareness (which in-

variably leads to the appreciation of music at deeper levels of the psyche).

3. To investigate the application of guided imagery to related fields such as visual/auditory research, music therapy, counseling, music appreciation, psychodrama, and religious experiences.

Using guided imagery in music therapy may have the following results in both individuals and groups: a more rapid surfacing of psychodynamic material; a means of getting beyond certain defense mechanisms; a stimulation of affect release; a facilitation of consciousness expansion; an enhancement of the possibility of transpersonal experience; and a fusion of mind and body awareness. In light of this enhancement of music therapy techniques, the following exercises* in guided imagery are presented in this chapter: the responsive instrument (Bonny & Savary, 1973); group fantasy (Bonny & Savary, 1973); group grounding (Bonny & Savary, 1973); and tribal dance (Bonny & Savary, 1973).

THE RESPONSIVE INSTRUMENT

Purpose of the Activity

To allow group members to reach and explore nonordinary levels of human consciousness.

To encourage imagination and interpretive skills.

To provide less verbal group members with an activity in which they may participate more fully.

To provide a means of expression.

*From *Music and Your Mind: Listening With a New Consciousness* by Helen L. Bonny and Louis M. Savary.
Copyright © 1973 by Collins Associate Publishing Inc.
Reprinted by permission of Harper & Row, Publishers, Inc.

To expose group members to different kinds of music.

To promote socialization via group interaction and cooperation.

To provide a self-satisfying and positive experience.

Procedure for Action

This exercise is based on the "mood iso principle," which states that "at the beginning of a listening experience, best results are obtained when the mood of the music matches the mood of the listener." (p. 43) As the exercise progresses, however, the direction is always geared toward a positive mood. Therefore music is chosen to depict the general mood of the group. The group is told, "Just as the musician must contribute the proper mood and intensity to any performance, so the instrument must be responsive to the performer. Only when performer and instrument work together is true music created" (Benny & Savary, 1973, p. 64).

The group is instructed that in this exercise they must try and identify with the instruments played by the soloist or orchestra, while letting the music slowly work its way into each one of them. The therapist may help the group in this procedure by making the following suggestions:

> Imagine the melody and movement of the music entering your heart: Let it be pumped into your body through your arteries and veins. Watch the mood and rhythm of the music fill your bloodstream. As the arteries deep in the body send their content into the capillaries on the surface of the skin, and the sensitive skin begins to respond with tingling reactions, you know that the instrument is ready to respond to the performer. Imagine yourself physically turning into the instrument you wish to become. Perhaps you wish to be the keyboard of a piano, the strings of a guitar, the bow of a violin, the bell of a trumpet. The music will suggest what is most appropriate for you. It may take a few moments to become accustomed to your new role as instrument, so give your body-mind plenty of time to feel at home in its new role. Enjoy the feeling of performing as an instrument, totally

cooperating with the performer. This is a very deep sharing space, especially if you can relate through feelings to your performer. When the piece is completed, return to your normal consciousness (Bonny & Savary, 1973, pp. 64–65).

In addition to having everyone share their experiences, the therapist should point out to the group that with practice they may be able to asume the roles of both instrument and performer, even interchangeably within the same experience. And since they are all the composers of their own experiences, they can even become composer, performer, and instrument simultaneously. These ideas may be further discussed.

Rules Governing Action

To be determined with each group.

Number of Required Participants

One or more.

Roles of Participants

To become completely involved in the exercises.

Results or Payoff

Reaching a higher level of consciousness, and possibly improving one's musicianship.

Abilities and Skills Required for Action

Cognitive—auditory perception, imagination, and interpretation.

Sensory-motor—the ability to communicate, preferably by talking.

Affective—the ability to relate to oneself as well as to others.

Interaction Patterns

Intra-individual, aggregate, intra-group.

Physical Setting and Environmental Requirements

A large, comfortable floor area with no intruding stimuli.

Required Equipment

Tape recorder and tapes.

GROUP FANTASY

Purpose of the Activity

To help group members reach and explore nonordinary levels of human consciousness.

To promote socialization via group interaction and cooperation.

To provide a means of communication and expression.

To encourage imagination and interpretive skills.

To expose group members to different kinds of music.

To provide a positive and self-satisfying experience.

Procedure for Action

Everyone should be lying on their backs in a circle, with their heads pointing toward its center in a star formation, while holding hands. Music is played softly enough so that the participants can hear one another easily.

After the music is begun, someone in the group spontaneously starts the fantasy by telling everyone what he or she sees (in the mind's eye) and feels. When this person thinks he has described his fantasy enough for others to enter it, he squeezes a neighbor's hand to signal the transfer of the opportunity to develop the fantasy. This continues until someone decides that the fantasy is complete. Enough time, however, should be allowed for the fantasy to unfold in detail.

The symbols and images that occur over and over in the group during the activity will provide material for discussion and analysis after the exercise. Upon completion of the exercise, the person who felt that the fantasy was completed suggests that everyone brings themselves "back to the present" and open their eyes after a one-two-three count.

Rules Governing Action

To be determined with each group.

Number of Required Participants

One or more.

Roles of Participants

To become completely involved in the exercises.

Results or Payoff

Reaching a higher level of consciousness.

Abilities and Skills Required for Action

Cognitive—auditory perception, imagination, and interpretation.

Sensory-motor—the ability to communicate by talking.

Affective—the ability to relate to oneself as well as to others.

Interaction Patterns

Intra-individual, aggregate, intra-group.

Physical Setting and Environmental Requirements

A large, comfortable floor area with no intruding stimuli.

Required Equipment

Tape recorder and tapes.

GROUP GROUNDING

Purpose of the Activity

To help group members reach and explore nonordinary levels of human consciousness.

To promote socialization via group interaction and cooperation.

To encourage imagination and interpretive skills.

To provide less verbal group members with an activity in which they may participate more fully.

To provide a means of nonverbal communication.

To expose members to different kinds of music.

To provide a positive and self-satisfying experience.

Procedure for Action

This exercise is used to build group unity and energy. A short exercise in "groaning and toning" (a technique for relaxing and inducing altered consciousness involving vocal and physical action) is recommended as a lead-in to this activity (and is effective at the start of any session). "Peak experience music" (music that is exciting and vigorous) should be used.

As the music begins, the therapist asks the group to be physically "in touch with something that grounds them in reality," for example, by holding onto another person. It should be made clear that it is acceptable to begin alone. Explain to the group that when grounded, one feels free to "go into far-off spaces" (to let go of ordinary consciousness), yet feels confident of being "anchored" to reality. Meanwhile, the therapist brings the participants together by physically leading them toward one another, speechless, so that after 20 or 30 minutes all the members of the group are in the middle of the room "tied together" by holding hands. The therapist should not, however, rush those still deep into their personal experiences, but should return after a few minutes when they are ready to join the group.

Rules Governing Action

No verbal communication is allowed during the activity.

Number of Required Participants

Four or more.

Roles of Participants

To become completely involved in the exercises.

Results or Payoff

To reach a higher level of consciousness.

Abilities and Skills Required for Action

Cognitive—auditory perception, imagination, and interpretation.

Sensory-motor—the ability to be physically joined with the rest of the group.

Affective—the ability to relate to oneself as well as to others.

Interaction Patterns

Intra-individual, aggregate, intra-group.

Physical Setting and Environmental Requirements

A large, comfortable floor area with no intruding stimuli.

Required Equipment

Tape recorder and tapes.

TRIBAL DANCE

Purpose of the Activity

To help group members reach and explore nonordinary levels of human consciousness.

To promote socialization via group interaction and cooperation.

To provide a means of communication and expression.

To encourage imagination, creativity, and interpretive skills.

To expose group members to different kinds of music.

To provide a positive and self-satisfying experience.

Procedure for Action

This exercise is used to build group energy through group movement. An exercise in movement or "groaning and toning" (see previous activity) is suggested as a lead-in to this activity.

The music chosen should have an intense strong beat (suggesting tribal dance), and should be long enough and interesting enough to allow for an assortment of body movements and group reactions.

As the music begins, the group members (who have been taking part in the "groaning and toning" exercise) are asked to respond to the music in physical motion. Since the exercise is unstructured, they may move alone, in pairs, or in groups. However, they should become aware of their togetherness and shared strength as the energy level among them increases. This may lead to everyone doing the same motion in unison while holding onto one another.

Rules Governing Action

To be determined with each group.

Number of Required Participants

Four or more.

Roles of Participants

To become completely involved in the exercises.

Results or Payoff

Reaching a higher level of consciousness and bringing people closer together

Abilities and Skills Required for Action

Cognitive—auditory perception, imagination, creativity, and interpretation.

Sensory-motor—the ability to move one's body to the music as one feels it.

Affective—the ability to relate to oneself as well as to others.

Interaction Patterns

Intra-individual, aggregate, intra-group.

Physical Setting and Environmental Requirements

A large, comfortable floor area with no intruding stimuli.

Required Equipment

Tape recorder and tapes.

Chapter 15

MUSIC THERAPY IN THE COMMUNITY

Although the community mental health movement is not a new phenomenon, it was not until 1963, under Public Law 88164, that Congress appropriated funds to be used toward constructing comprehensive mental health centers proposed within the framework of state mental health plans. Since then, outpatient services have been established in a variety of settings: community day centers (a meeting place for clubs composed of released patients); outpatient psychiatric clinics (a unit that provides outpatient mental health services and has a position for a psychiatrist who has regularly scheduled hours in the clinic, and who assumes medical responsibility for all patients); the five-day hospital (a program set up in many institutions to allow and even encourage their patients to go home on the weekends); the night hospital (a psychiatric unit that offers treatment to patients after working hours); the open hospital (which allows increased freedom to the mental hospital ward, where patients are helped to manage their new freedom, find some useful work to do, and plan a more constructive use of their leisure time);

family therapy (a specific therapy for the emotional disorders of the family group, and a method for improving the harmful forms of an individual's emotional interactions with his family); foster families (for expatients who do not need to be in hospitals but who cannot return to their own families or live on their own); physical rehabilitation centers (programs and treatment of the physically disabled, such as Easter Seals Rehabilitation Centers, Lighthouse Centers for the Blind, Cerebral Palsy Centers, schools for the auditorally impaired, special classes for learning-disabled and brain-damaged children, and speech therapy in public schools); drug rehabilitation centers (residential treatment centers to help drug abusers overcome their addiction, continue their education, and find employment); residential centers for disabled children (a program that provides 24-hour care in a therapeutic milieu, integrating education, group living, group therapy, and clinical treatment, allowing the possibility of extensive family involvement in the treatment program, and facilitating the return to full community living by easily arranged transitions to day or night services and by using regular school facilities as the child improves); and, finally, special schools, classes, and workshops for persons with all disabilities.

Music therapy has a place in all of these settings—whether exercises are made more bearable for the physically disabled through the use of music; retarded children acquire self-help skills via musical games; drug addicts learn about the responsibility, hard work, and joys of putting on a musical production; emotionally disturbed persons find a means of communication and emotional release in an instrumental combo; or outpatients find a way to use their leisure time and a place to socialize as members of a choir or at a dance.

No matter what other goals are set in therapy, the end goal is usually community involvement—a return to full community living. Since most of this book already deals with many of the music therapy activities that can be provided in the community, this chapter will deal with activites that may help the individual make the transition back into full community living. The activities presented in this chapter are: plans after discharge (Wolfe et al, 1975); hobbies (Wolfe et al., 1975); weekends (Wolfe et al., 1975); situations (Wolfe et al., 1975); responsibility (Wolfe et al., 1975); leading a session (Wolfe et al., 1975).*

PLANS AFTER DISCHARGE

Purpose of the Activity

To encourage the making of specific, concrete discharge plans, and to encourage ideas and feedback from other group members.

To encourage socialization via verbal interaction and co-operation in a group setting.

To promote independent thinking and decision making.

To encourage concentration and on-task behavior.

To provide a positive, productive experience.

Procedure for Action

Group members are instructed to make a list of specific, concrete, realistic plans they hope to have fulfilled after discharge into the community. Each member then selects a song that he feels describes one of the plans on the list, plays it for the group, and explains why that plan was chosen and the relationship of the song to it.

Group discussion may center around the following questions: Is it important to have fairly concrete plans for discharge, and why? Are your plans realistic? What programs does the community have to offer? What job opportunities are available? The therapist should do some preliminary research on what the

*Activities are included by permission of David Wolfe from *Analysis of Music Therapy Group Procedures,* Golden Valley Health Center, Minneapolis, 1975.

community actually has to offer each member of the group such as day centers, the "Y," and adult education.

Rules Governing Action

None.

Number of Required Participants

Three or more.

Roles of Participants

To make a list of plans, choose an appropriate song for one of them and participate actively in the discussions.

Results or Payoff

Aid in making appropriate discharge plans, improvement of independent thinking and decision-making skills, and helpful feedback from others.

Abilities and Skills Required for Action

Cognitive—concentration, independent thinking, and the ability to make decisions.
Sensory-motor—the ability to communicate.
Affective—the ability to work well with others.

Interaction Patterns

Intra-individual, aggregate, intra-group.

Physical Setting and Environmental Requirements

Any setting that is comfortable and available for meeting.

Required Equipment

An assortment of recordings and a record player.

HOBBIES

Purpose of the Activity

To encourage group members to examine their present abilities and skills.

To motivate members to acquire new hobbies.

To encourage socialization via verbal interaction and co-operation in a group setting.

To provide a self-satisfying and positive experience.

Procedure for Action

Group members are instructed to make a list of all of the hobbies they once had, presently have, or would like to acquire. Each group member then selects a song that describes one of these hobbies, plays it for the group, and explains why it was chosen and the relationship of the song to the hobby. The rest of the list is read and written on a blackboard, so that one large list is formed from all the lists of the group.

Group discussion may center around the following questions: Do you think hobbies are important, and why? How were your hobbies acquired? Do you have any hobbies that you have been neglecting, and why? Where do you think you can acquire new hobbies in the community? Are you interested in any of the hobbies written on the blackboard? The therapist should do some preliminary research on what the community actually has to offer each group member.

Rules Governing Action

None.

Number of Required Participants

Three or more.

Roles of Participants

To make a list of hobbies, to choose a song representing one of them, and to participate actively in discussion.

Results or Payoff

Reviving a neglected hobby, finding out about acquiring a new one, and sharing ideas about hobbies already acquired.

Abilities and Skills Required for Action

Cognitive—convergent thinking.
Sensory-motor—the ability to communicate.
Affective—the ability to work well with others.

Interaction Patterns

Intra-individual, aggregate, intra-group.

Physical Setting and Environmental Requirements

Any setting that is comfortable and available for meeting.

Required Equipment

Various records, a record player, and a blackboard and chalk.

WEEKENDS

Purpose of the Activity

To promote socialization via verbal interaction and cooperation in a group setting.

To give group members feedback from other members concerning weekend experiences.

To help members examine alternate means of handling situations that arise over weekends, and to discover positive things to do.

To provide a positive, productive experience.

Procedure for Action

Each group member is instructed to select a song that describes his or her experiences, something learned or enjoyed, over the past weekend. After the playing of each song, the group member explains how the song relates to the weekend, and group discussion is encouraged.

Here are some possible discussion questions: Did you spend your weekend doing positive things? Would you rather have done something else? Did you experience anything that you felt you had difficulty handling? What are some positive things you could do next weekend? What does the community have to offer as inexpensive alternatives? The therapist should do some preliminary research on inexpensive community programs, exhibits, shows, and so on.

Rules Governing Action

None.

Number of Required Participants

Three or more.

Roles of Participants

To select a song that describes their weekend and to participate actively in the discussions.

Results or Payoff

To find more positive ways to spend a weekend.

Abilities and Skills Required for Action

Cognitive—convergent thinking.
Sensory-motor—the ability to communicate.
Affective—the ability to work well with others.

Interaction Patterns

Intra-individual, aggregate, intra-group.

Physical Setting and Environmental Requirements

Any setting that is comfortable and available for meeting.

Required Equipment

An assortment of recordings and a record player.

SITUATIONS

Purpose of the Activity

To present a variety of situations, reactions resulting from these situations, and ways to deal with these situations and reactions.

To promote independent thinking and problem solving.

To encourage socialization via verbal interaction and co-operation in a group setting.

To provide a positive, productive experience.

Procedure for Action

Each group member is given a card that describes a realistic life situation with the instruction to try to imagine himself or herself in the position described. For example, "At your new job, some people you work with are going out together after work, and they've asked you to join them. How do you feel?" Each member then selects a song that describes the way he or she might react in this given situation, plays it for the group, and either explains what reaction the song represents or has the group try to guess. The situations given should be realistic ones so that the discussion will be meaningful in helping the group members deal with potential or actual situations in their lives. Discussion may center on differing and common reactions to the same situation, and on ways of dealing with the reactions and the situation.

Rules Governing Action

None.

Number of Required Participants

Three or more.

Roles of Participants

To imagine one's reaction to a situation, find a song that describes the reaction, and actively participate in the discussions.

Results or Payoff

Greater awareness of one's reactions to situations and possible ways in which to deal with both.

Abilities and Skills Required for Action

Cognitive—independent thinking and problem solving.
Sensory-motor—the ability to communicate.
Affective—the ability to work well with others.

Interaction Patterns

Intra-individual, aggregate, intra-group.

Physical Setting and Environmental Requirements

Any setting that is comfortable and available for meeting.

Required Equipment

An assortment of recordings and a record player.

RESPONSIBILITY

Purpose of the Activity

To expand the group's concept of responsibility to include internal as well as external factors.

To promote independent and rational thinking.

To make group members more aware of the possible differences between reality and their thoughts or emotions.

To promote socialization via verbal interaction and cooperation in a group setting.

To provide a positive, productive experience.

Procedure for Action

Each member selects a song that describes his or her concept of responsibility, plays it for the group, tells how it relates to responsibility, and joins the group in discussion. Or the therapist may play songs that relay the concept of responsibility (such as Helen Reddy's "Best Friend" and Cat Stevens' "Father and Son"), and then opens up the discussion by asking, "How does this song describe responsibility?" Besides external factors such as one's job and home life, the discussion should deal with internal factors—for example, testing one's emotions and thoughts against reality, using positive thoughts to help oneself, even comparing internal responsibility (morals, ethics) with external responsibility (job, finances). Responsibility for one's own well-being may be overlooked as a responsibility by the group and should then be pointed out by the therapist (especially in relation to therapy, medication, and so on) as unobtrusively as possible.

Rules Governing Action

None.

Number of Required Participants

Three or more.

Roles of Participants

To select a song describing the concept of responsibility and actively participate in the discussions.

Results or Payoff

Deeper insight into the internal and external factors of responsibility.

Abilities and Skills Required for Action

Cognitive—divergent, convergent, and independent thinking, and insight and reason.

Sensory-motor—the ability to communicate.

Affective—the ability to relate to oneself as well as to others.

Interaction Patterns

Intra-individual, aggregate, intra-group.

Physical Setting and Environmental Requirements

Any setting that is comfortable and available for meeting.

Required Equipment

An assortment of recordings and a record player.

LEADING A SESSION

Purpose of the Activity

To provide the opportunity for each group member to take the responsibility of planning and leading a session or part of a session.

To provide the opportunity for group members to respond to the direction of a peer.

To promote socialization via verbal interaction and cooperation in a group setting.

To provide an insightful experience.

Procedure for Action

It may help to complete the previous exercise on responsibility with the group before doing this activity. Group members are encouraged to lead a future session, but none should be forced to; a member may be directly asked by the therapist, chosen by the group, or volunteered. On the chosen day, the group member leads the session with an activity he or she has planned, and the therapist participates as another group member. The group member is responsible for everything that happens during the activity (within reason).

It may be necessary for the therapist to conduct a previous session dealing with the preliminaries of planning an activity and carrying it out, discussing goals, methods, equipment, and so on. Discussions should focus on giving the group member constructive feedback and on drawing parallels between the responsibilities of leading a session and those of leading one's life, and of being a group member and of being a member of a community

Rules Governing Action

None.

Number of Required Participants

Four or more.

Roles of Participants

To plan and lead a session, or to participate as a regular group member in whatever activity is being done.

Results or Payoff

The opportunity to experience the responsibility of planning and leading an activity.

Abilities and Skills Required for Action

Cognitive—divergent and convergent thinking.
Sensory-motor—the ability to communicate.
Affective—the ability to relate to others.

Interaction Patterns

Intra-individual, aggregate, intra-group.

Physical Setting and Environmental Requirements

Any setting that is comfortable and available for meeting.

Required Equipment

Depends on the activity led by the group member.*

*Actually, all of these categories depend on the activity led by the group member. The analysis made deals with the activity of planning and leading a session.

Chapter 16

MUSIC THERAPY AND
TRANSACTIONAL ANALYSIS

The method psychotherapy called transactional analysis (TA) originated with the psychiatrist, Dr. Eric Berne, who developed it between 1950 and his death in 1970. This procedure examines the transaction wherein "I do something to you and you do something back" and determines which part of the multiple-natured individual is "coming on." The three parts (or ego states) of this multiple nature (or personality) are: the "parent" ego state (which contains the attitudes and behaviors incorporated from external sources, primarily parents); the "adult" ego state (which is oriented to current reality and the objective gathering of information); and the "child" ego state (which contains all the impulses that come naturally to the infant).

One of the most important developments of this method is the systematization of the information derived from analyzing these transactions in words that have the same definition for everyone using them. With an emphasis on group treatment, one of the main objectives of TA is to help an individual become aware of these three parts of his personality so that he will become better able to make decisions regarding future behavior and the future course of his life.

TA is concerned with four types of analysis: structural analysis (the analysis of individual personality); transactional analysis (the analysis of what people do and say to one another); game analysis (the analysis of ulterior transactions leading to a payoff); and script analysis (the analysis of specific life dramas that persons compulsively play out). A "script" (or tape) is a personal life plan decided on by each individual at an early age in reaction to his interpretations of external events. These early decisions are called "life positions," and there are four of them according to Berne (1961):

1st. Position:	I'M OK—YOU'RE OK
Translation:	life is worth living
	(this is a potentially healthy position)
2nd. Position:	I'M OK—YOU'RE NOT OK
Translation:	your life is not worth much
	(the projective position)
3rd. Position:	I'M NOT OK—YOU'RE OK
Translation:	my life is not worth much
	(the introjective position)
4th. Position:	I'M NOT OK—YOU'RE NOT OK
Translation:	life isn't worth anything at all
	(the futility position) (p. 269)

All transactions can be classified as complementary (when a message, sent from a specific ego state, gets the predicted response from a specific ego state in the other person); crossed (when an unexpected response is made to the stimulus, causing a breakdown in communication); or ulterior (when a message is disguised under a socially acceptable transaction, but is really meant to be sent by another ego state). Two concepts that occur as a result of crossed transactions are "exclusion," which involves either one ego state being in control most of the time or the shutting-off of one or more ego states; and "contamination," which is characterized by an adult ego state that holds as fact certain ideas stemming from the parent or child ego states. Ulterior transactions involve game playing.

According to Berne (1961), there are six ways in which people spend their time: withdrawal (when one is alone with one's thoughts, all alone in a room or in a room filled with people); rituals (when everyone agrees to do the same thing according to social standards, without commitment or involvement or really communicating); activities (when something useful is accomplished); pastimes (when one is just passing time); games (when one says one thing but really means something else); and intimacy (when two people accept the "I'm OK, you're OK" position).

TA is a contractual form of treatment between the client and the therapist: The client specifies the change that is desired, and the therapist indicates acceptance (or rejection) of the contract to facilitate this change and the conditions under which this will be achieved. Unless the client desires additional changes, the treatment relationship is ended when the contract has been fulfilled.

Arnold (1975) has found parallels between the concepts of music therapy and TA, "suggesting that music as a physiological language and a psychological language has the potential to cathect the child ego state; provide a structure for stroking, fun, permission, awareness, and intimacy; and to serve as a unifying factor in a session designed to deal with the problem of structuring time" (p. 105). ("Permission" is a therapeutic operation in script analysis which allows an individual to change his decision to follow parental injunctions, and thus to take charge of his own life.) In view of Arnold's findings, this chapter presents various activities that incorporate music therapy in a transactional analysis setting (designed by the author and former colleagues, 1975).

Purpose of the Activity

To make group members more aware of their parent, adult, and child ego states.

To bring about self-esteem via self-actualization.

To promote socialization via group interaction and cooperation.

To enjoy as many satisfying transactions as possible with other group members.

Gradually to increase involvement, participation, and group cohesiveness.

To provide another means of verbal and nonverbal communication.

To provide a structure for stroking, fun, permission, awareness, and intimacy.

Procedures for Action

Many activities can be devised to incorporate music therapy into TA. Here are a few:

Have each group member find a partner. Explain that when the music begins, one member of each pair is to begin moving in one of the ego states (P, A, or C) without any verbal indication to the other member of the pair about which state it is. The other member, meanwhile, is to react in movement to the music and the ego state which he or she believes the partner is in. Have the partners discuss their reactions to the music and each other, analyzing their transaction, first between themselves and then with the rest of the group.

A variation of this procedure is to give the group the following directions: "Listen to the music and move (1) as you did when you were a child, (2) as your parents would have liked you to move, (3) as you think you should move, (4) as your parents would have moved, or (5) as you feel like moving right now." Music that can fit any of these states is selected, and discussion of the movements and what they represent is encouraged afterwords.

Another movement activity is called "The OK Polka" (or "Disco" or any other dance that is most appropriate for the group). The group forms subgroups of six members each, and printed cards are made for each group: Three have verbal statements representing P, A, or C; and three have written physical actions representing P, A, or C. The goal of each group is to match parent action to parent statement, adult action to adult statement, and child action to child statement. Groups members are allowed to do only what is on their specific cards. When they find their match, they say "I'm OK, you're OK" to each other. The partners then begin dancing to the polka being played. The winning group is the one that has all its partners dancing first, that is, the first group that completes all its complementary transactions.

Several rounds may be conducted, but group discussion should be encouraged after each one. This activity is related to a game that is played with children. The children make a circle around the therapist, whose eyes are closed, and sing this song:

> Can you guess who I am? AM I a P, A, or C?
> Can you guess who I am? Why don't you wait and see?

When they stop singing, the therapist (whose eyes are still closed) points to one of the children, who must do a P, A, or C action (for example, foot stamping, yelling, thumb sucking, finger shaking, decision making, or calmly talking). The child who correctly guesses which state it is gets to go into the middle of the circle. If no one can guess correctly, the child who performed the action goes into the center of the circle. Each child should be given a chance to perform an action, and the actions should be discussed.

In another game the group is divided into two teams, and each team chooses a captain. On separate pieces of paper, each team writes titles of songs, musicals, or operas, and the type of transaction (for example, "Button Up Your Overcoat"—parent to child) or life position (for example, "I Am A Rock"—I'm Not OK, you're Not OK) each title represents. Using the rules of Charades, the other team must guess the titles and transactions or life positions within a time limit. The team that guesses them in the least amount of time wins.

Another game calls for the group to be divided into three subgroups: one is P, one is A, and one is C. Each of these groups is to think of song lyrics that describe the characteristics of each of these states. One of the groups begins by singing the lyrics that describe one of the other groups, and this group must respond by singing lyrics that describe another, and so on. The goal is to keep the transactions going complementarily as long as possible. Score may be kept by giving points to the group that stumps the other two. The last group to sing begins a new transaction.

Music may also be analyzed in terms of TA. One approach is to write song lyrics out as a script, and have each group member take parts and read the lyrics as if they were a play. The actual recording is heard and a discussion is held on whether the group members agree on the way the lyrics were assigned to P, A, or C. Another approach is to play recordings for the group, some with contradictory words and music, others with words and music that agree (for example childish music and adult words, or adult music and adult words). The group members analyze the words and music for each selection and discuss whether they feel the words and music agree or disagree.

In any discussion involving music therapy and TA, the therapist may point out that just as people are different, so are their musical tastes and interpretations. And, just like a song, a person has different "states," which, if recognized, can be changed. All of these activities are designed on the premise that the group has been familiarized with TA concepts and methods.

Rules Governing Action

Rules depend on the specific activities and contracts.

Number of Required Participants

Six or more.

Roles of Participants

To be aware of the different actions and characteristics of the P, A, and C states in themselves and others.

Results or Payoff

Fulfillment of one's contract.

Abilities and Skills Required for Action

Cognitive—auditory perception, role playing, insight.

Sensory-motor—the ability to move all different parts of one's body and to communicate.

Affective—the ability to relate to one's feelings as well as those of others, and to work well with others, especially in such a dynamic situation.

Interaction Patterns

Intra-individual, aggregate, intra-group, inter-group.

Physical Setting and Environmental Requirements

A large, open floor area.

Required Equipment

An assortment of recordings and a record player, paper and pencils, and possibly tapes, a tape recorder, and instruments.

Chapter 17

DEVELOPMENTAL MUSIC THERAPY

Developmental therapy, as formulated by Dr. Mary Wood, Associate Professor at the University of Georgia, is a psycho-educational treatment approach based upon patterns of sequential growth and development of two- to 14-year-old children who have severe emotional or behavioral disorders. The developmental music therapy program incorporates the principles of music therapy into the developmental approach.

The program provides a series of music therapy experiences, based on the philosophy of the Orff-*Schulwerk* approach, that are designed to compliment and enhance the existing development of these children. This model draws from the fields of psychiatry, psychology, social work, education, and music education.

The standard changes and growth sequences in the development of children are used to move them through the therapeutic process. Children are grouped not by their chronological ages, but according to their stage of development, in four curriculum areas: behavior, communication, socialization, and academics. These areas are divided into five developmental stages, and each stage requires certain behaviors of the child and the music therapist. The role of the music therapist, the amount of therapeutic intervention required, the types of music therapy experiences needed, and the amount of participation by the child changes with each stage; and each child progresses through these stages at varying rates. The program concentrates on the development of each child's musical potential by devising therapeutic musical experiences appropriate for each child's level of functioning in the four areas. (See Purvis, J., and Sament, S. (Eds.), *Music in Developmental Therapy.)*

Chapter 18

MUSIC THERAPY AND MUSIC EDUCATION

There are many similarities between music therapy and music education. Both fields have similar goals and techniques; even their "clients" are similar in many ways. The main concern of both fields is to achieve the highest possible levels of human behavior among their clients. The main difference lies in the use of music itself. Music education attempts to develop artistic, or aesthetic, activity and attitudes in musical behaviors; music therapy uses such artistic activities and attitudes to help persons develop the most human behavior patterns of which they are capable. While music education is concerned with perfecting musical endeavor and music as a product, music therapy is concerned with eliciting changes in behavior *via* music.

However, the music therapist can put the music lesson to therapeutic use. Once an individual begins playing a piece of music, he must perform each tone at the proper time with the correct pitch, dynamics, and duration, and, in an ensemble, in the proper combination with the other tones. Such musical behavior is ordered by reality, so the therapist is provided with objective evidence of how appropriately the individual is reacting to the real stimuli of the printed and sounded music.

Many disabled individuals compensate for their handicaps via musical participation. Here lie opportunities for socially acceptable praise or criticism and enhancement of pride in self, as well as a means of self-expression, a means of experiencing successful endeavors, and a way to gain the esteem and respect of others.

Most musical participation takes place within groups, which offer opportunities for accepting responsibility for oneself and others, developing self-directed and other-directed behavior, experiencing cooperation and competition in socially acceptable ways, enhancing verbal and nonverbal communication and social interaction, learning realistic social skills and personal behavior patterns, and enjoying leisure-time activities in recreation and entertainment.

The music lesson can be structured to achieve such therapeutic goals as an increase in attention span; an increase in memory recall; the development of perceptual-motor coordination; the development of imagination and creativity; an increase in auditory/perceptual awareness; the development of body orientation; the utilization of different body parts; the development of such concepts as discrimination and generalization; as well as other goals already mentioned.

Whether the instruction is instrumental, vocal, or theoretic, or lessons in music appreciation, under the leadership of a skilled teacher-therapist these musical activities can help disabled individuals attain the most competent, most socially acceptable, and most gratifying human behavior patterns of which he or she is capable.

Chapter 19

MUSICAL PRODUCTIONS

The development and performance of a musical production is a dynamically stimulating event in the social life of a school or institution, or even in a community: Its effects reach through the audience as well as the participants. When a production of any sort is created and then brought to life by its creators, the performance transmits their capacities for care, perception, and cooperation to the audience, who also experience the commitment and sense of fulfillment of these participants. As the individualities of the participants are actively expressed, their disabilities take a second place, and may even become nonexistent during the presentation. Such a production can often reveal undetected abilities and other aspects of the personalities of the participants, which can be informative to staff members and families.

For the participants the performance is the consummation of a series of developing experiences. Some may have found freedom from their disabilities by learning to use new skills; others may have developed some carefulness or confidence in self-expression. During the development of the production, participants may learn of compromises but still feel satisfaction in the finished product. The actual performance and the applause it receives bring the feelings of self-esteem and self-assurance. And through all the preparation, the actual performance, and cleaning up afterwards, a cohesiveness develops among the participants which lays the foundation for future interactions and the development of productive social skills.

A "musical production" may consist of only a cassette tape recording of a song or instrumental combo, or it may be a videotape of an actual concert; it may be a light show with music in the background, or the musical talents may become the center of attention in a talent show; it may even be a full-fledged musical, with plot, scenery, and costumes. The actual content becomes important only in how it is used: As with teaching music in therapy, the production itself is the means, not the end. In another sense, though, the musical production is the culmination of all therapeutic efforts by all participants including the staff.

Chapter 20

PSYCHIATRIC MUSICOLOGY

The use of musicological methods in clinical psychiatry was developed by Johanna Stein (1974), from her observation of the music and speech patterns of "regressed chronic patients whose social behavior was largely absent or repetitively stylized" (p. 110). According to Stein, these patients produced music that appeared to be "full of mistakes," but when analyzed "turned out to be individually stable musical reorganizations whose forms resembled the form, not the content, of their creators' behavior" (p. 110).

Upon request, the psychiatric musicologist meets with staff-patient treatment groups to listen for, identify, and interpret patients' non-communicative but self-expressive speech. When patients are referred by physicians, evaluations are made on the basis of the patients' patterns of "defensive mis-perception" of various musical structures in order to assess the patients' problem areas. (Psychiatric and psychological methods of assessment requiring verbal responses are limited in their evaluations because of the extent of impairment in these pa-

249

tients' verbal communication.) Information acquired from formal analysis of "defensive elements" in the patients' spontaneous musical compositions, and about the patients' perception and use of their speaking and singing voices, are additional factors in the patients' evaluations.

On the basis of these assessments, the psychiatric musicologist confers with the patients' primary clinical staff to formulate practical treatment plans. When this primary clinical staff refers patients, the psychiatric musicologist designs and carries out ancillary music therapy. Patients whose defensiveness about verbal communication is likely to impede verbal forms of therapeutic intervention are offered musical activities structured to facilitate communication. Patients are treated individually or in small groups.

In addition to diagnositc and clinical services, the psychiatric musicologist may provide technical consultation services to nursing assistants, mental health counselors, and other staff involved with the therapeutic use of music in assessing and treating patients.

Based on formal analogies between details of musical structure and interpersonal events, rather than on any content equivalency, Stein (1974) maintains that translating perceptual errors in music in to clinical information is technically possible. She reports that patterns of altered perception in various categories of mental illness differ a great deal from one another, and that diagnostic differences far exceed individual differences. Of the several hundred patients examined by Stein, wide variability in social class, age, race, religion, education, and musical ability and training were irrelevent to the perceptual errors (1974).

APPENDIX A

Films*

Are You Ready?

This film shows the activities (including the music therapy activities) of a group of children with Down's syndrome in a prescriptive teaching program (based on the Illinois Test of Psycholinguistic Abilities) in sequence of difficulty. The execution of the nine measurable areas of the ITPA are broken down for research purposes. The effectiveness of prescriptive teaching with this group of children is shown after two years of structured experiences at the Orchard School for Special Education in Skokie, Illinois. This film is recommended for any group concerned with care, planning, and education for children with Down's syndrome, including teachers, therapists, school administrators, physicians, nurses, parents, and legislators.

*All films are available through NAMT, Inc., PO Box 610, Lawrence, KS. 66044.

A Breathing Therapy for Pulmonary Emphysema

In this film the Musicians Emergency Fund provides a therapist, Joseph Florestano, to demonstrate exercises in breath management for emphysema sufferers in Saint Albans Naval Hospital in Long Island, New York. This film is recommended for doctors, hospitals, research centers, clubs, schools, and other interested organizations.

Child at the Gate

A study in music, art, and poetry therapies with an adult schizophrenic woman, this film shows in depth the experiences of this severely depressed, withdrawn patient who was referred to the Music Therapy Center in New York City when she was 27. She had withdrawn from all contact into a "self-protective seclusiveness" since childhood, and hospitalized in mental institutions 20 times since the age of 17. This film shows how communication begins in music therapy; how a trusting and secure relationship is established; how symbolic communication (via the arts or interpersonal behavior) is accepted, understood, and responded to by the therapists; and how the patient's combined experiences in the three ongoing arts therapies enable her to integrate her ego, to move out of her inner world, to relate to others, and to take her place in the real world to an extent never before possible. This film is recommended for educational and clinical training and is not appropriate for showing to the general public.

David School: A Communication-Learning Program for Non-Verbal Psychotic Children

This film highlights the school day of two boys, ages five and six years, one with no speech and the other with beginning speech, at the David School of the Michael Reese Hospital's Dysfunctioning Child Center. It shows work with simultaneous communication (signing and speech), music, table tasks, and group games. Teaching video tapes are also available. This film is recommended for any audience.

I Can't Hear, But I Can Sing

In this film, the integration of the hearing-impaired into the classroom via music and sign language is described by Helen Mandel Grob as part of the interdisciplinary clinical training program for music therapists at the Mental Retardation Institute of the New York Medical College. The film is intended solely for music therapy training directors and students, and for those involved in programs for the auditorily impaired. It is not appropriate for showing to the general public.

The I in the Beat

This film shows how music therapy is used in a public special education class, with emphasis on the discovery of self through music and the dynamic group process. Therapy is geared toward the child's emotional, physical, and intellectual needs as each experiences rhythm, sound, sight, and movement through total sensory exploration. Each experience is shown to provide a wealth of accomplishments, which helps the child build self-confidence and develop the courage to explore new avenues, which in turn strengthen the learning process. This film is intended solely for the professions dealing with exceptional children (especially the mentally retarded) and is not appropriate for showing to the general public.

Listen to the Music Makers

This is a documentation of a project sponsored by the Department of Health and Welfare in Ottawa to demonstrate the music therapy techniques used throughout the greater Vancouver area. The film shows two music therapists using improvisation techniques to stimulate and enrich children with various growth and learning handicaps in a preschool for special children. The film is intended primarily for working professionals and parents, but it can also be understood by high school teenagers.

The Mikado Is Coming

This film deals with the teamwork involved in helping a group of physically handicapped children put on a presentation of the operetta, "The Mikado." It shows some of the problems that had to be overcome in preparing the production, as well as actual scenes from the completed presentation. This film would be appropriate to show to university students and general adult audiences.

Moving True

This film demonstrates the use of dance therapy with a severely withdrawn female patient in a condensation of dance therapy sessions at the Music Therapy Center in New York City. A one-to-one relationship between a dance therapist and the patient was necessary for the patient to express herself freely and fully in a physical way, without harm to herself or to others. As trust and rapport developed over the sessions, and through the technique of mirroring the patient's actions (relating on a physical level), a basic working relationship evolved (relating on an emotional level). This film presents the challenge posed by a special patient with strong needs, and is recommended for college and professional groups. It is not appropriate for showing to the general public.

Music and Your Mind: A Key to Creative Potential

The Guided Imagery and Music technique is presented in this documentary as two subjects, an actress and a concert pianist, are taken through the music listening experience by an experienced guide. The procedure is explained briefly to allow the audience an inside view of what takes place when selected music stimuli are administered to relaxed subjects. To explore consciousness from the point of view of psychodynamics, creativity, and oceanic or peak experience, the film uses live performance as well as taped music. This film is recommended for persons involved in or training for clinical practice, the performing arts, education, creative arts therapies, research, or depth psychology.

The Music Child

This documentary shows how improvised music is used as a treatment technique for achieving communication with nonverbal children who are either autistic, emotionally disturbed, or mentally retarded, or who have cerebral palsy. Vera Moretti, Beverly Parry, the late Dr. Paul Nordoff, Clive Robbins, and other music therapists jointly narrate the film, explaining their own personal techniques and strategies, and appearing in the demonstration of them. This film, a winner in the American Film and International TV festivals, is recommended for the therapist, parent, classroom teacher, layman, and musician interested in music as a treatment approach to the handicapped child.

Music Therapy

This film was designed to provide an introductory understanding of the basic concepts of music therapy, and to begin to sensitize students to the methods and practice of the music therapist. As such, the film is recommended highly for high school juniors and seniors, beginning students in music therapy, and adult groups who wish to become familiar with the goals and practice of music therapy.

Music Therapy Internship

Narrated by the late Dr. E. Thayer Gaston, former president of the National Association for Music Therapy, this film (1) describes the purposes and plan of therapeutic procedures, (2) shows music therapy interns conducting a variety of music therapy activities with mentally retarded children, and (3) discusses the content of the three- and six-month internships in music therapy at Parsons State Hospital. In view of this, the film is recommended for undergraduate music therapy students, music therapists, hospital staffs, and professional organizations interested in mental retardation.

Music With A Capital T

This film depicts a day in the life of a music therapist. Not for individual use, this film is recommended for organizations and schools.

Organized to Serve

Past state and local presidents of the Association for Children With Learning Disabilities are featured in this film, along with a music therapist, to discuss the value of recreation and learning through music therapy; a teen canteen; summer camp; and the public service role of the ACLD, telling parents how to communicate with their schools. Part IV of the series, "All Children Learn Differently," this film is recommended for those individuals interested in the education of the learning disabled.

Reach Inside

This film shows the use of music activities in the classroom to assist the growth of learning disabled and educable retarded pupils. Although music therapy processes or the potential of music therapy in special education is not shown, techniques that music therapists might employ are demonstrated (for example, Orff and Kodály techniques are demonstrated by resource consultants Mary H. Richards and Martha Wampler). Because of the nature of this film, it is recommended for college and professional groups.

A Song for Michael

At 14 years of age, Michael has no spontaneous speech. His medical history includes a diagnosis of autism, schizophrenia, brain damage, and mental retardation. He has an attention span of only a few minutes and is given to frequent outbursts of motor activity. After 10 years of treatment through various therapies and special education, Michael is referred to the Music Therapy Center in New York City. This film concentrates on one session between Michael and his music therapist, dealing exclusively with music therapy and the many possibilities of its use with the exceptional child. It is solely intended for professional audiences and is not appropriate for showing to the general public.

VIDEOTAPES*

Accountability in Music Therapy

The "accountability approach" is illustrated in music therapy with the mentally retarded in relation to the ethics, standards, behavioral objectives (clinical and administrative), evaluation, and illustration of performance. The tape is therefore recommended especially for music therapists, special

*All videotapes are available through NAMT, Inc., PO Box 610, Lawrence, KS. 66044

educators, and other professionals who work with the mentally retarded.

Instrument and Vocal Music Performance in Music Therapy

With an emphasis on social skills in therapy, this tape shows the preparation and performances of the Pinecrest performing groups: the bell choirs; combo; drum corps; vocal ensemble; and square, folk, and modern dancers. This tape is recommended for music therapists, special educators and other professionals who work with the mentally retarded.

Music Therapy in Mental Retardation

This tape covers aspects of music therapy programs for the mentally retarded; programs in the Pinecrest music therapy department; and discussions and illustrations of music therapy techniques in motor development, activities of daily living, communication skills, social-emotional development, development of self-concept, and conceptual skills. The tape is recommended for music therapists, special educators, and other professionals who work with the mentally retarded.

Music Therapy Workshop I

Edited from actual sessions in music therapy, this tape covers the development of motor and self-care skills via music therapy activities with the severely and moderately retarded in a residential setting. This tape is recommended for music therapists, special educators, and other professionals who work with the mentally retarded.

Music Therapy Workshop II

Edited from actual sessions in music therapy, this tape covers the development of self-concept, communication skills, social skills, and conceptual skills through music therapy activities with the severely and moderately retarded in a residential setting. This tape is recommended for music therapists, special educators, and other professionals who work with the mentally retarded.

Processes in Music Therapy

Abstracted from Gaston's (1968) book *Music in Therapy,* this tape presents music therapy activities that illustrate the theory and processes in music therapy practice with the mentally retarded. This tape is recommended for music therapists, special educators, and other professionals who work with the mentally retarded.

The Sounds They Make: Music in Therapy

The role of the Registered Music Therapist in all treatment of the mentally retarded and the mentally ill is examined in this tape. Simulated music therapy sessions demonstrate their effects in treating a behaviorally disordered adolescent, in teaching social and academic skills to a trainable mentally retarded girl, and in promoting transferable music skills with a community mental health center patient.

As a member of a therapeutic team, a professional music therapist takes part in analyzing the problems of individual patients and in establishing treatment goals before planning and carrying out specific musical activities. In addition, an evaluation session is recreated where such a team accounts for the success or failure of the procedures used. Also discussed is the balance between academic and clinical training in the educational preparation of music therapists.

Because of the content of this tape, it is recommended for undergraduate music therapy students, music therapists, hospital staffs, and professional organizations interested in mental health.

Recordings*

American Game and Activity Songs

Pete Seeger, Folkways #7002, (LCR-62-1498).

Recommended especially for very young children.

Basic Concepts Through Dance (Body Image)

Album EALP 601, 33-⅓ rpm.

Recommended for the development and reinforcement of self-concepts in children who are mentally retarded and/or physically handicapped with neurological impairments.

Basic Concepts Through Dance (Position in Space)

Recommended for the development and improvement of perceptual-motor skills.

Canadian Folk Dances

Selected and edited by Eileen Reid; Bowmar Educational Records.

Recordings of Canadian dances with instructions included.

Carpet Square

MH 31, 33-⅓ rpm.

Recommended for the development of basic motor skills, balance, corrdination, and dexterity (via carpet squares).

---

*All recordings are available through the various companies listed (see Appendix C). When no company is listed for a specific recording, that recording is available from various companies.

Children's Dances Using Rhythm Instruments

LP 9078, album or cassette with manual.

Familiar, simple dances that can be done seated or standing, with authentic or improvised instruments.

Come Dance with Me

Two LP albums (Nos. HLP-3078 and HLP-3078-1) with teaching booklet and various other accompanying aids.

Basic principles of rhythm and movement are explored via music.

Coordinated Classroom Activities Through Movement, Music, Art

LP 7030, album or cassette with manual.

Music activities include specific behavioral objectives, such as static and dynamic balance, and locomotor skills. Movement activities include a group game with all kinds of gallops, creative movement for balance, and movements included on the Neurological Gait Examination. Art activities encourage this total learning experience.

Dances of Hawaii

Bowmar Educational Records.

Nine ancient and modern dances of the South Seas with directions and information in a separate booklet.

Dances Without Partners

Educational Activities, Inc.

Easy-to-do group dances that feature the individual.

Developing Perceptual-Motor Needs of Primary-Level Children

Album AR 606-7, two 33-⅓ rpm records.

A sequentially developed training program for the establishment of perceptual-motor skills.

The Development of Body Awareness and Position in Space

Album AR 605, 33-⅓ rpm.
Educational Activities, Inc.

A researched, sequentially developed training program for the establishment of accurate body awareness and position in space.

Developmental Motor Skills for Self Awareness

LP 9075, album or cassette with manual.

Concepts for development of self-expression activity via dance therapy techniques, language skills, and art.

Dubka

Rashid Records, 191 Atlantic Avenue, Brooklyn, NY 11201.

Mid-Eastern music and dances with dance directions.

Eight 18th-Century Dances

PR 699 (Nos. 1–4), PR 700 (Nos. 5–8).
Paxton Records.

Dances by Desmond MacMahon with dance instructions.

Eight Swiss Dances

PR 711 (Nos. 1–4), PR 712 (Nos. 5–8).
Paxton Records.
Dances by Desmond MacMahon with dance instructions.

Festival Folk Dances

RCA (LPM-1621).
Includes such dances as the Highland fling, the hornpipe, and the ribbon dance.

Finger Games

Album HYP 506, 33-⅓ rpm.
Rhythmic verses combined with hand motions.

First Folk Dances

RCA (LPM-1625).
Includes such dances as Polly Wolly Doodle, Kinder-polka, The Wheat, and Dance of Greeting.

Folk Dances for All Ages

RCA (LPM-1622).
Includes such dances as the schottische and the Norwegian Mountain March.

Folk Dances for Fun and All-Purpose Folk Dances

RCA (LPM-1624) and RCA (LPM-1623).
Two companion albums to "First Folk Dances."

Folk Dances of the World

Hoctor Dance Records, Inc.

Dances from Israel, Greece, Sweden, Mexico, Ireland, Italy, Hungary, Turkey, Poland, and Yugoslavia with instructions.

Folkcraft Records

1159 Broad Street, Newark, NJ 07102.

Series of international folk dance accompaniments.

4008 Elementary School Exercises to Music

Record 4008V (vocal instructions); record 4008NV (music only).

Hoctor Dance Records.

Exercise routines to well-known tunes with instructions.

French Game Songs

Bowmar Educational Records, M-107.

Songs by Rith DeCesare (book separate).

Fun Activities for Fine Motor Skills

LP 9076, album or cassette with manual.

Rhythmic activities and exercises that focus on the development of fine motor skills.

Get Fit While You Sit—Grades 3–8

Album AR 516, 33⅓ rpm.

Muscle strengthening, fitness, and coordination activities

are presented in a way that also enhances listening skills, auditory perception, and aural memory; talk-through ... do-through instructions, complete imaginative routines, and illustrated manual included.

Hap Palmer Record Library

Canadian–Educational Media.

A series of records, cassettes, books, and guides that offer modern and enjoyable approaches to all aspects of child development.

Happy Folk Dances

RCA (LPM-1620).

Recommended folk dances for junior high school ages.

The Hokey Pokey

MH 33, 33-⅓ rpm.

Different tunes and tempos with complete instructions.

Latin-American Game Songs

Bowmar Educational Records, M-104.

Songs by Ruth DeCesare (book separate).

Learning Basic Skills Through Music

Volume I (AR 514), Volume II (AR 522), 33-⅓ rpm with manuals or cassette; also available in Spanish.

Rhythmic teaching program of numbers, colors, the alphabet, body awareness, telling time, and reading readiness.

Learning Basic Skills Through Music-Building Vocabulary

EA 521, 33-⅓ rpm.

Learning safety vocabulary, kinds of foods, parts of the body, forms of transportation, and objects around the room via active participation; learning the concepts of forward-backward, inside-outside, high-low, over-under-around via simple, original game songs.

Let's Square Dance

Richard Kraus, RCA series 3000–3004.

A how-to-do-it series of five albums with illustrated instructions accompanying each album.

Listen, Move and Dance

Vols. 1 and 2 (H-21006 and H-21007).
Capital Records.

Listening and Moving: Relaxation (Impulse Control Through Relaxation)

AR 655, 33-⅓ rpm.

Activities that show ways to utilize muscular activities to decrease levels of stimulation and increase muscular control via oral instructions and music.

Listening and Moving: Simple Agility Movements for Impulse Control (Pre-Tumbling Skills)

AR 656, 33-⅓ rpm.

Relaxation training that promotes body image and impulse control as well, via basic tumbling movements.

Mexican Folk Dances

Bowmar Educational Records.

Six popular Mexican dances with instructions.

Multi-Purpose Singing Games

EALP 510, 33⅓ rpm.

Recommended for relieving tension via large body movements while also helping listeners develop listening skills; teaching body awareness, handedness, coordination, and agility; and encouraging interpretive dramatic expression.

Multi-Purpose Singing Games #2

EALP 511, 33-⅓ rpm.

Longer-action singing games than #1 to further encourage listening, coordination, spontaneity, rhythm, and dramatic expression.

1,2,3, and Move

(Today's Rhythms for Basic Motor Skills and Today's Melodies for Rhythmic Activities)

LP 9077, two albums or cassettes with manual.

Album I consists of original music to accompany such basic skills as skipping, galloping, marching, tiptoeing, jumping, and hopping; album II consists of popular songs arranged for gymnastics exercises, dance trampolines, ball bouncing, singing, and clapping.

Physical Fitness for All Grades: Body Conditioning Teen Adults

A. B. LeCrone Company.

Thirty body conditioning exercises in 25 minutes.

Physical Fitness for All Grades: For Intermediate Grades

A. B. LeCrone Company (RRC-903 record).

Sixteen physical exercises and deep breathing exercises in 15 minutes.

Physical Fitness for All Grades: For Preschool and Kindergarten

A. B. LeCrone Company (RRC-703).

Twenty physical exercises and deep breathing exercises in 15 minutes time; adult direction not needed.

Physical Fitness for All Grades: For Primary Grades

A. B. LeCrone Company (RRC-803).

Rhythmic songs for 16 physical exercises and deep breathing exercises in 15 minutes; no adult aid needed.

Play Party Games

Decca Records, AL278.

Favorite and familiar singing games such as "Skip to My Lou."

Play Party Games

Bowmar Educational Records.

Two albums of three records, each containing many traditional singing games; written instructions included.

Popular and Folk Tunes for Dancing and Rhythmic Movement

HLP 4074.

Recommended for teaching the development of conscious

body control and a conscious response to music, and for providing a joyous or calming atmosphere.

Rhythmrix: Grade 4–High School

Album AR 31, two 33-⅓ rpm records with manual.

Eight rhythmic drills of body movement in a continuous series of physical exercises done in time to different musical accompaniments.

Rhythms for Children (Call and Response)

Ella Jenkins, Folkways (FC7308).

Group singing and drum rhythms, and rhythm chants.

Rhythms for Today

Album HYP 29, two 33-⅓ rpm records.

Updated, familiar rhythms, sounds, and experiences with written rhymes for chanting in time to the music; there are over 50 bands divided into natural movements, movable objects, body movements, make-believe people, animals, nature, real people, travel, space travel.

Simplified Folk Dance Favorites

Album EALP 602, 33-⅓ rpm.

Recommended for the mentally retarded and physically handicapped learning to develop physical skills, social abilities, and a sense of emotional well-being from successful achievement; dances repeated at three tempos.

Singing Action Games

Album HYP 507, 33-⅓ rpm.

Neither partners nor learning specific steps and movements are required, since participants are encouraged to use their imagination and ability to pretend.

Singing Games and Folk Dances

Bowmar Educational Records.
A series of revised editions:
"Singing Games," albums 1 and 2
"Singing Games and Folk Dances," album 3
"Folk Dances" (from around the world), album 4
"Folk Dances" (American), album 5
"Folk Dances" (Latin-American), album 6

Singing Square Dances

Bowmar Educational Records.
Three albums with verbal instructions before each dance and a "singing" caller with the music.

Sometime-Anytime Songs

Washington Records (WC-303).
Imaginative songs with musical interludes for response.

Songs and Rhythms From Near and Far

Folkways #7655 (LCR-64-343).
Original songs in English by Ella Jenkins which introduce folk rhythms from Canada, Greece, Syria, and other countries.

Square Dances

Folkways #2001 (LCR-58-728).
Calls and music to both Eastern and Western dances.

Square Dancing Made Easy

Columbia LN 3607.

Fourteen square dances with directions and terminology.

26 All-Purpose Action Tunes

HLP-4068/69, two LP records.

A variety of activities which may be used for games, skipping, running, walking, dancing (ballet or tap), exercises, rhythm band, or music appreciation.

The World of Folk Dances

Michael Herman, RCA.

A series, each with directions:
    "First Folk Dances," LPM-1625
    "Folk Dances for Fun," LPM-1625
    "All-Purpose Folk Dances," LPM-1623
    "Folk Dances for all Ages," LPM-1622
    "Festival Folk Dances," LPM-1621
    "Happy Folk Dances," LPM-1620
    "Special Folk Dances," LPM-1619.

APPENDIX B

INTERACTION PATTERNS

Following is a list of the interaction patterns defined in Avedon's model (Columbia, 1971).

> Intra-individual: individual only, action within mind or body; no contact with outside object or other person.
> Extra-individual: action directed person to object in environment, but no contact is necessary with other person.
> Aggregate: activity directed by person toward object in environment while others do same thing in same environment: parallel play.
> Inter-individual: activity of competitive nature which is directed from one person to another.
> Unilateral: activity of competition between three or more persons, one of whom is antagonist or "it."
> Multilateral: activity of competition among three or more people, no one is it, everyone competes.
> Intra-group: action of cooperation by two or more who are interested and intent upon reaching a goal, requires positive verbal and nonverbal interaction.
> Inter-group: competition among two intra-groups.(pp. 424–425)

APPENDIX C

CREATIVE ARTS THERAPY ORGANIZATIONS

A.I.M., Inc. (Adventures in Movement for the Handicapped)
945 Danbury Road
Dayton, Ohio 45420

American Art Therapy Association, Inc. (AATA)
3607 South Braeswood Boulevard
Houston, Texas 77025

American Association for Music Therapy (AAMT)
Department of Music and Music Therapy of New York University
35 West Fourth Street—777 Education Building
New York, New York 10003

American Dance Therapy Association (ADTA)
Suite 230, 200 Century Plaza Building
Columbia, Maryland 21044

American Orff Schulwerk Association (AOSA)
Post Office Box 18495
Cleveland Heights, Ohio 44118

American Society of Group Psychotherapy and Psychodrama
39 East Twentieth Street
New York, New York 10003

Association for Poetry Therapy
799 Broadway, Suite 629
New York, New York 10003

British Society for Music Therapy
48 Lancaster Road
London, N. 6, England

Canadian Association for Music
Therapy (CAMT)
6 Drayton Road
Pointe Claire, Quebec H9S 4V2
Canada

Coordinating Office for the Regional
Resource Centers
University of Kentucky
East Wing, Kinkead Hall
University Station
Lexington, Kentucky 40506

The Dalcroze Society, Inc.
89, Highfield Avenue
London, NW11 9TU, England

Information and Research Utiliza-
tion Center
Physical Education and Recreation
for the Handicapped
American Association for Health,
Physical Education and Recreation
1201 Sixteenth Street, N.W.
Washington, D.C. 20036

Institute for Consciousness and Music (ICM)
721 Saint Johns Road
Baltimore, Maryland 21210

Kodály Musical Training Institute,
Inc.
525 Worcester Street
Wellesley, Massachusetts 02181

Music Educators National Conference (MENC)
1202 Sixteenth Street, N.W.
Washington, D.C. 20036

National Association for Music
Therapy, Inc. (NAMT)
Post Office Box 610
Lawrence, Kansas 66044

National Therapeutic Recreation Society (NTRS)
National Recreation and Park Association
1601 Kent Street
Arlington, Virginia 22209

Therapeutic Recreation Information
Center (TRIC)
Department of Recreation and Park
Management
University of Oregon
1607 Agate Street
Eugene, Oregon 97403

MATERIAL AND EQUIPMENT SUPPLIERS

Audio House
307 East Ninth Street
Lawrence, Kansas 66044

Blocks,
1330 North Drive,
Memphis, Tennessee 38109

Bowmar Records, Inc.
622 Rodier Drive
Glendale, California 91201

Canadian Educational Media, Ltd.
185 Spadina Avenue, Suite 1
Toronto, Ontario M5T 2C6 Canada

Canadian Folk Dance Record Service
605 King Street, West
Toronto 28, Ontario, Canada

Century Records Manufacturing Company
Century Custom Recording Service
Post Office Box 308
Squgus, California 91350

Children's Music Center, Inc.
5373 West Pico Boulevard
Los Angeles, California 90019

Custom Fidelity Record Company
222 East Glenarm Street
Pasadena, California 91101

Educational Activities, Inc.
Post Office Box 392
Freeport, New York 11520

The Empire Music Company, Ltd.
934 Twelfth Street
New Westminister, British Columbia, Canada

Festival Records
161 Turk Street
San Francisco, California 91402
or
2769 West Pico Boulevard
Los Angeles, California 90006

Folk Dance House
108 West Sixteenth Street
New York, New York 10011

Folkcraft
1159 Broad Street
Newark, New Jersey 07114

Folklore Imports
4220 Ninth Avenue, N.E.
Seattle, Washington 98105

Folkways Records
701 Seventh Avenue
New York, New York 10036

Golden Records
Affiliated Publishers
630 Fifth Avenue
New York, New York 10020

Herco Products, Inc.
53 West 23rd Street
New York, New York 10010

Hoctor Dance Records, Inc.
Post Office Box 38
Waldwick, New Jersey 07463

M. Hohner Inc./Sonor
Andrews Road
Hicksville, New York 11802

Ken-Del Productions, Inc.
Custom Record Division
111 Valley Road
Richardson Park
Wilmington, Delaware 19804

Kimbo Educational
Post Office Box 246A
Deal, New Jersey 07723

Kid Stuff
(see Master Musical Instruments,
Inc.)

A. B. LeCrone Rhythm Record
Company
819 N.W. 92nd Street
Oklahoma City, Oklahoma 73114

Lyons
530 Riverview Avenue
Elkhart, Indiana 46514

Magnamusic-Baton, Inc.
6390 Delmar Boulevard
St. Louis, Missouri 63130

Manhassett Specialty Company
Post Office Box 2518
Yakima, Washington 98902

Master Musical Instruments, Inc.,
Post Office Box 3681
Centerline, Michigan 48015

Melody Cradle Company
1502 South Twelfth Street
Goshen, Indiana 46529

Melody House
819 N.W. 92nd
Oklahoma City, Oklahoma 73114

Mitchell Manufacturing Company
2740 South 34th Street
Milwaukee, Wisconsin 53246

Music Education Group (MEG)
1415 Waunegan Road
Northbrook, Illinois 60062

Music in Motion
Post Office Box 5564
Richardson, Texas 75080

Musik Innovations
Box One
Allison Park, Pennsylvania 15101

Myklas Music Press
Post Office Box 929
Boulder, Colorado 80306

Peripole Products, Inc.
51-17 Rockaway Beach Boulevard
Rockaway, Long Island, New York
11691

Pine Tree Records
Rod Linell
Peru, Maine 04272

QT Records
Statler Record Corporation
73 Fifth Avenue
New York, New York 10003

Radio-Matic of America, Inc.
760 Ramsey Avenue
Hillside, New Jersey 07205

RCA Records
1133 Avenue of the Americas
New York, New York 10003

The Record Center
1614 North Pulaski
Chicago, Illinois 60607

Remo, Inc.
12804 Raymer Street
North Hollywood, California 91605

Rhythm Band, Inc.
Post Office Box 126
Fort Worth, Texas 76101

Rhythms Products Records
Whitney Building, Box 34485
Los Angeles, California 90034

Rico Corporation
Post Office Box 5028, Bendix Station
North Hollywood, California 91605

Ruth Evans
Box 132, Post Office Branch X
Springfield, Massachusetts 01107

School Specialties
48 West Northfield Road
Livingston, New Jersey 07039

Schulmerich Carillons, Inc.
Carillon Hill
Sellersville, Pennsylvania 18960

Selmer Company, The
Box 310
Elkhart, Indiana 46514

Shawnee Press, Inc.
Delaware Water Gap
Pennsylvania 18327

Society for Visual Education, Inc.
1345 Diversey Parkway
Chicago, Illinois 60614

Studio 49 (see Magnamusic-Baton, Inc.)

Summit Industries
Post Office Box 415
Highland Park, Illinois 60035

Trophy Music Company
Division of Grossman Music Corporation
1278 West Ninth Street
Cleveland, Ohio 44113

Twelgrenn, Inc.
Box 216
Bath, Ohio 44210

Vogt Quality Recordings
Post Office Box 302
Needham, Massachusetts 02192

Volkwein Brothers, Inc.
117 Sandusky Street
Pittsburgh, Pennsylvania 15212

Wenger Corporation
90 Park Drive
Owatonna, Minnesota 55060

BIBLIOGRAPHY

BOOKS

Abramson, R. M. *Rhythm games.* New York: Music & Movement Press, 1973.

Alvin, J. *Music for the handicapped child,* London: Oxford University Press, 1965.

Alvin, J. *Music Therapy.* New York: Basic Books, 1974.

Apel, W. *Harvard Dictionary of Music,* London: Heinemann Educational Books, Ltd., 1969.

Apprey, Z. R., Apprey, M. *Applied music therapy: Collected papers on a technique and a point of view.* London: Institute of Music Therapy and Humanistic Psychology, The International University, 1975.

Bailey, P. *They can make music.* London: Oxford University Press, 1973.

Balazs, E. *Dance therapy in the classroom.* Waldwick, NJ: Hoctor Products for Education, 1977.

Batcheller, M. J., Mansour, S. *Music in recreation and leisure.* Dubuque, Iowa: William C. Brown Company Publishers, 1972.

Berne, E. *Games people play.* New York: Grove Press, 1964.

Berne, E. *Transactional analysis in psychotherapy.* New York: Grove Press, 1961.

Berne, E. *What do you do after you say hello?* New York: Grove Press, 1972.

Bernstein, D., & Borkover, T. *Progressive relaxation training.* Champaign, Illinois: Research Press, 1973.

Bernstein, P. L. *Theory and methods in dance-movement therapy.* Dubuque, Iowa: Kendall/Hunt Publishing Company, 1972.

Bernstein, P. L. (Ed.) *Eight theoretical approaches in dance–movement therapy.* Dubuque, Iowa: Kendall/Hunt Publishing Company, 1979.

Birkenshaw, L. *Music for fun, music for learning,* Toronto: Holt, Rinehart and Winston, 1974.

Bitcon, C. H. *Alike and different: The clinical and educational use of Orff-Schulwerk.* Santa Ana, California: Rosha Press, 1976.

Bonny, H. L., & Savary, L. M. *Music and your mind.* New York: Harper & Row, 1973.

Bright, R. *Music in geriatric care.* New York: St. Martin's Press, 1972.

Chaiklin, H. (Ed.). *Marian Chace: Her papers.* Columbia, MD: The American Dance Therapy Association, Inc: Marian Chace Memorial Fund, 1975.

Chosky, L. *The Kodály Method.* Englewood Cliffs, NJ: Dell Publishing Co, 1973.

Dalcroze, E. J. *Rhythm, music and education,* H. F. Rubenstein (trans.). Aylesbury Bucks, Great Britain: Hazell, Watson and Viney, 1921.

"Dance Therapy." *Maryland/Washington, DC/Virginia ADTA Chapter's Symposium,* March 14, 1975.

Deaver, M. J. *Sound and silence.* Pikeville, Kentucky: Curriculum Development and Research, 1975.

Dobbs, J. P. B. *The slow learner and music.* London: Oxford University Press, 1966.

Dorian, M. *Ethnic Stories for children to dance,* USA: BBB Associates, 1978.

Driver, A. *Music and movement,* New York: Oxford University Press, 1943.

Dutoit, C. L. *Music movement therapy.* London: Riverside Press, 1971.

Edwards, E. M. *Music education for the deaf.* South Waterford, Maine: The Merriam-Eddy Company, 1974.

Findlay, E. *Rhythm and movement: Application of Dalcroze eurhythmics.* Evanston, Illinois: Summy-Birchard Company, 1971.

Gadling, D., Porkny, D. H., & Rickehof, M. (Eds.). *Lift Up Your Hands,* Washington, D.C., The National Grange, 1976.

"Game." *The World Book Encyclopedia Dictionary,* 1964, I, 815.

Gaston, E. T. (Ed.). *Music in therapy.* New York: The Macmillan Company, 1968.

Geiger, J. A. *Adventures in movement for the handicapped.* Dayton, Ohio: Adventures in Movement, 1976.

Ginglend, D. R., Stiles, W. E. *Music activities for retarded children.* Nashville: Abingdon Press, 1965.

Graham, R. *Music for the exceptional child.* Restor, Va: Music Educators National Conference, 1975

Harbert, W. K. *Opening doors through music: A practical guide for teachers, therapists, students, parents,* Springfield, Illinois: C. Thomas Co., 1974.

Jacobsen, E. *Progressive relaxation.* Chicago: University of Chicago Press, 1938.

Jones, B., & Hawes, B. L. *Step it down.* New York: Harper & Row, 1972.

Jones, G. *Seeds of movement.* Pittsburgh; Volkwein Brothers, 1976.

Jones, G. *Movement in the right direction: Experiences for anyone from 6 to 86.* Pittsburgh: Volkwein Brothers, 1979.

Keynton, T. *Homemade musical instruments,* New York: Drake Publishers, 1975

Kramer, E. *Art therapy in a children's community.* Springfield, Illinois: Thomas, 1958.

Landis, B., & Carder, P. *The Eclectic curriculum in American Music Education: Contributions of Dalcroze, Kodály & Orff,* Washington, D.C.: Music Educators National Conference, 1972.

Leedy, J. J. *Poetry therapy.* Philadelphia: L. B. Lippincott, 1969.

Marsh, M. *Explore and discover music.* New York: Macmillan Publishing Company, 1970.

Materials on creative arts for persons with handicapping conditions, Washington, D.C.: Association for Health, Physical Education & Recreation, 1975.

Moreno, J. *Psychodrama.* New York: Beacon House, 1946.

Moreno, Z. T. *Psychodramatic Rules, Techniques and Adjunctive Method.* New York: Beacon House, 1966.

Nash, G. *Creative approaches to child development with music, language and movement.* Port Washington, NY: Alfred Publishing Company, 1974.

Nordoff, P., & Robbins, C. *Music therapy for handicapped children.* New York: Rudolf Steiner Publications, 1965.

Nordoff, P., & Robbins, C. *Music therapy in special education.* New York: The John Day Company, 1971.

Nordoff, P., & Robbins, C. *Creative music therapy.* New York: The John Day Company, 1976.

Paynter, J., & Aston, P. *Sound and silence: Classroom projects in creative music.* London: Cambridge University, 1970.

Postl, J., & Yaross, L. *Music for children: A Carl Orff workshop guide.* Chicago, Illinois: O.S.P.I.—Department for Exceptional Children, 1976.

Priestly, M. *Music therapy in action.* New York: St. Martin's Press, 1975.

Prince, L. *Movement sound and reading readiness.* River Forest, Illinois: Prince Publications, 1975.

Prince, L. *Movement and sound, for exceptional, for young children.* River Forest, Illinois: Prince Publications, 1976.

Purvis, J., & Sament, S. (Eds.). *Music in developmental therapy: A curriculum guide.* Baltimore: University Park Press, 1976.

Roberts, R. *Musical instruments made to be played.* Leicester England: Dryad Press, 1969.

Robins, F., Robins, J. *Educational rhythmics for mentally and physically handicapped children.* New York: Association Press, 1968.

Role of music in the special education of handicapped children. The conference proceedings, April 5 & 6, 1971, SUNY, the State Education Department, Albany, NY, 1971.

Schafer, R. M. *Creative Music Education,* New York: Schirmer, 1976.

Schoop, T. *Won't you join the dance?.* Palo Alto, California: National Press Books, 1974.

Steiner, R. *Eurhythmy,* London: Steiner Press, 1967.

Tomat, J., Krutzky, C. *Learning through music for special children and their teachers.* South Waterford, Maine: Merriam-Eddy Co., 1975.

Ulman, E. & Dachinger, P. *Art therapy in theory and practice.* New York: Schocken Books, 1975.

Wagner, B. J. *Dorothy Heathcote: Drama as a learning medium.* Washington, D.C.: National Education Association of the United States, 1976.

Wakefield, E. E. *Folk dancing in America.* New York: J. Lowell Pratt, 1966.

Ward, D. *Hearts and hands and voices.* London: Oxford University Press, 1976.

Wheeler, L., Raebeck, L. *Orff and Kódaly adapted for the elementary school.* Dubuque, Iowa: William C. Brown Company, 1972.

Whethered, A. G. *Movement and drama in therapy.* Boston Plays, Inc. 1973.

Williams, P. *Making musical instruments,* London: Mills & Boon, 1971.

Wolfe, D. E., Burns, S., Stoll, M., Wichmann, K., *Analysis of music therapy group procedures.* Minneapolis: Golden Valley Health Center, 1975.

Wuytack, J. *Musica Viva.* Paris: Alphonse Leduc, 1972.

Wuytack, J., Aaron, T.: *Joy, play, sing, dance.* Paris: Alphonse Leduc, 1972.

ARTICLES

Ainlay, G. W. The place of music in military hospitals. *Music in medicine.* D. M. Schullian & M. Schoen (Eds.). New York: Books for Libraries Press, 1948.

Altshuler, I. A. The value of music in geriatrics. *Music therapy,* 1959, 109–115.

Arnold, M. Music therapy in a transactional analysis setting, *Journal of Music Therapy,* 1975, *12,* 104–120.

Avedon, E. M. The structural elements of games, In E. M. Avedon & B. Sutton-Smith (Eds.), *The study of games,* New York: John Wiley & Sons, 1971.

Bang, C. Schulwerk with the deaf and multi-handicapped. In *Multi-choice notes for the 11th conference of the American Orff-Schulwerk Association.* Washington, D.C.: American Orff-Schulwerk Association, 1977.

Bang, C. *A music therapy event.* Hicksville, NY: M. Hohner, Inc., 1979.

Bixler, J. Operetta production with physically handicapped children. *Music Therapy,* 1960, 101–104.

Bixler, J. Music therapy practices for the child with cerebral palsey. In E. Thayer Gaston (Ed.). *Music in Therapy.* New York: The Macmillan Company, 1968, 143–151.

Boenheim, C. The importance of creativity in contemporary psychotherapy. *Journal of Music Therapy,* 1967, *4,* 3–6.

Bonny, H. L. Music and consciousness. *Journal of Music Therapy,* 1975, *13,* 121–135.

Brooking, M. Music therapy in British mental hospitals. *Music therapy,* 1959, 38–46.

Browne, H. E., & Winkelmayer, R. A structured music therapy program in geriatrics. In E. Thayer Gaston (Ed.). *Music in therapy,* New York: The Macmillan Company, 1968, 285–289.

Brunner-Orne, M., & Flinn, S. S. Music therapy at Westwood Lodge. *Music therapy,* 1960, 44–46.

Burnett, M. The Orff process: Applications for early childhood. In *Multi-choice notes for the 11th conference of the American Orff-Schulwerk Association.* Washington D.C.: American Orff-Schulwerk Association, 1977.

Campbell, D. D. One out of twenty: The Ld. *Music Educators Journals,* 1972, *April,* 22–23.

Castellano, J. A. Music composition in a music therapy program. *Journal of Music Therapy.* 1969, *6,* 12–14.

Chace, M. Report of a group project. St. Elizabeth Hospital. *Music Therapy.* 1954, 187–190.

Clemetson, B. C., & Chen, R. Music therapy in a day-treatment program. In E. Thayer Gaston (Ed.). *Music in therapy.* New York: The Macmillan Company, 1968, 394–400.

Cooke, R. M. The use of music in play therapy, *Journal of Music Therapy.* 1969, *6,* 66–75.

Crocker, D. B. Clinical experiences with emotionally disturbed children. In E. Thayer Gaston (Ed.). *Music in therapy.* New York: The Macmillan Company, 1968, 202–207.

Crocker, D. B. Music as a projective technique. *Music Therapy,* 1955, 86–97.

Crocker, D. B. Teaching piano to the young blind child. *Music Therapy,* 1956, 175–182.

Crocker, D. B. Techniques in the use of music as therapy for the emotionally maladjusted child. *Music Therapy,* 1952, 175–180.

Crocker, D. B. Using music in a speech therapy program. *Music Therapy,* 1958, 103–108.

Denenholz, B. Music as a tool of physical medicine. *Music Therapy,* 1958, 67–84.

Dickinson, M. Music as a tool in psychotherapy for children. *Music Therapy,* 1957, 97–104.

Douglass, D. R., Wagner, M. K. A program for the activity therapist in group psychotherapy. *Journal of Music Therapy,* 1965, *2,* 56–60.

Dreikurs, R., & Crocker, E. B. Music therapy with psychotic children. *Music Therapy,* 1955, 62–73.

Drier, J. C. Music therapy for exceptional children. *Music Therapy,* 1954, 124–130.

Fahey, J. D., & Birkenshaw, L. Bypassing the ear: The perception of music by feeling and touch. *Music Educators Journal,* 1972, *April,* 28–33.

Ficken, T. The use of song-writing in a psychiatric setting. *Journal of Music Therapy,* 1976, *13,* 163–172.

Flanders, F. R. A new music program for the mentally retarded child. *Bulletin of the National Association for Music Therapy, Inc.,* 1961, *10,* 7–8.

Fraser, L. W. Music therapy as a basic program for the handicapped child. In E. Thayer Gaston (Ed.). *Music in Therapy.* New York: The Macmillan Company, 1968, 87–95.

Fraser, L. W. The use of music in teaching writing to the retarded child. *Music Therapy,* 1960, 86–90.

Gibbons, A. The development of square dancing activity in a music therapy program at Rockland State Hospital. *Music Therapy,* 1956, 140–147.

Sister Giovanni. Music as an aid in teaching the deaf. *Music Therapy,* 1959, 88–89.

Goldstein, C. Music and creative arts therapy for an autistic child. *Journal of Music Therapy,* 1964, *1,* 235–238.

Goldstein, C., Lingas, C., & Sheafer, D. Interpretive or creative movement as a sublimation tool in music therapy. *Journal of Music Therapy,* 1965, *2,* 11–15.

Goodnow, C. C. The use of dance in therapy with retarded children. *Journal of Music Therapy,* 1968, *5,* 97–102.

Graham, R. M. Music therapy for the moderately retarded. In E. Thayer Gaston (Ed.). *Music in Therapy,* New York: The Macmillan Company, 1968, 78–86.

Graham, R. M. Seven million plus need special attention. Who are they? *Music Educators Journal,* 1972, *April,* 6–9.

Grenoble, B. The Schulwerk in special education. In *Multichoice notes for the 11th conference of the American Orff-Schulwerk Association.* Washington, D.C.: American Orff-Schulwerk Association, 1977.

Greven, G. M. Music as a tool in psychotherapy for children. *Music Therapy,* 1957, 105–108.

Griffin, J. E. Administration of a music therapy department in an institution for the mentally retarded—with suggested activities. *Journal of Music Therapy,* 1966, *3,* 99–105.

Haselbach, B. The aspect of "time" in movement, dance and music. In *Multi-choice notes for the 11th conference of the American Orff-Schulwerk Association.* Washington, D.C.: American Orff-Schulwerk Association, 1977.

Herman, F. K. Music therapy for children hospitalized with muscular dystrophy. In E. Thayer Gaston (Ed.). *Music in therapy.* New York: The Macmillan Company, 1968, 152–156.

Hollander, F. M., & Juhrs, P. D. Orff-Schulwerk, an effective tool with autistic children. *Journal of Music Therapy,* 1974, *11,* 1–12.

Johnson, L. W. In other words—Saying it with movement. In *Multi-choice notes for the 11th conference of the American Orff-Schulwerk Association.* Washington, D.C.: American Orff-Schulwerk Association, 1977.

Jorgenson, H., & Parnell, M. K. Modifying social behaviors of mentally retarded children in music activities. *Journal of Music Therapy,* 1970, *8,* 83–87.

Josepha, M. Music therapy for the physically disabled. In E. Thayer Gaston (Ed.). *Music in Therapy,* New York: The Macmillan Company, 1968, 110–135.

Josepha, M. Therapeutic values of instrumental performance for severely handicapped children. *Journal of Music Therapy,* 1965, *1,* 73–79.

Kenny, M. Intermediate/advanced process—development beyond the beginnings. In *Multi-choice notes for the 11th conference of the American Orff-Schulwerk Association.* Washington, D.C.: American Orff-Schulwerk Association, 1977.

Klingler, H., Peter, D. Techniques in group singing for aphasics. *Music Therapy,* 1962, 108–112.

Kozak, Y. A. Music therapy for orthopedic patients in a rehabilitative setting. In E. Thayer Gaston (Ed.). *Music in therapy.* New York: The Macmillan Company, 1968, 166–168.

Lathom, W. B. Application of Kodály concepts in music therapy. *Journal of Music Therapy,* 1974, *11,* 13–20.

Lathom, W. B. The use of music therapy with retarded patients. In E. Thayer Gaston (Ed.). *Music in therapy.* New York: The Macmillan Company, 1968, 66–77.

Lathom, W. B., Edson, S., & Toombs, M. R. A coordination speech therapy and music therapy program. *Journal of Music Therapy,* 1965, *2,* 118–120.

Levin, H. D., & Levin, G. M. Instrumental music: A great ally in promoting self-image. *Music Educators Journal,* 1972, *April,* 15–18.

Lewis, D. Chamber music—proposed as a therapeutic medium. *Journal of Music Therapy,* 1964, *1,* 19–20.

Leiderman, P. C. Music and rhythm group therapy for geriatric patients. *Journal of Music Therapy,* 1967, *4,* 126–127.

Lindecker, J. M. Music therapy in a juvenile detention home. *Music Therapy,* 1953, 108–114.

Matteson, C. A. Finding the self in space. *Music Educators Journal,* 1972, *April,* 47–49.

Maultsby, M. C. Combining music therapy and rational behavior therapy. *Journal of Music Therapy,* 1977, *14,* 89–97.

Michel, D. E. Music therapy in cleft-palate disorders. *Music Therapy,* 1961, 111–115.

Michel, D. E. Music therapy in speech habilitation of cleft-palate children. In E. Thayer Gaston (Ed.). *Music in therapy.* New York: The Macmillan Company, 1968, 162–166.

Mooney, M. K. Blind children need training, not sympathy. *Music Educators Journal,* 1972, *April,* 40–43.

Moreno, J. J. Musical psychodrama: A new direction in music therapy. *Journal of Music Therapy,* 1980, *17,* 34–42.

Music Therapy as a Career. Lawrence, Ks: The National Association for Music Therapy, Inc., 1977.

Nichols, E. L. Orff can work in every classroom. *Music Educators Journal,* 1970, *September,* 43–44.

Ostwald, P. F. The music lesson. In E. Thayer Gaston (Ed.). *Music in therapy.* New York: The Macmillan Company, 1968, 317–325.

Peterson, C. A. *Activity analysis and prescriptive programming: Purpose, procedures, applications.* East Lansing: Michigan State University, 1976.

Ponath, L. H., & Bitcon, C. H. A behavioral analysis of Orff-Schulwerk. *Journal of Music Therapy,* 1974, *11,* 147–155.

Price, R., Rast, L., & Winterfelt, D. Out of pandemonium—music! *Music Educators Journal,* 1972, *April,* 19–20.

Ragland, Z., Apprey, M. Community music therapy with adolescents. *Journal of Music Therapy,* 1974, *11,* 147–155.

Robison, D. E. Music therapy in a children's home. In E. Thayer Gaston (Ed.). *Music in therapy.* New York: The Macmillan Company, 1968, 208–214.

Robison, D. E. The withdrawn child and monotonism. *Bulletin of the National Association for Music Therapy,* 1963, *12,* 6–16.

Rogers, L. Music therapy in a state hospital for crippled children. In E. Thayer Gaston (Ed.). *Music in therapy.* New York: The Macmillan Company, 1968, 156–159.

Ruppenthal, W. "Scribbling" in music therapy. *Journal of Music Therapy,* 1965, *2,* 8–10.

Schneider, E. H. Music for the cerebral palsied child. *Music Therapy,* 1960. 97–100.

Seybold, C. D. The value and use of music activities in the treatment of speech delayed children. *Journal of Music Therapy,* 1971, *8,* 102–110.

Sharpe, N. Workers' music club. *Music Therapy,* 1962, 94–97.

Shrodes, C. Bibliotherapy. An application of psychoanalytic therapy. *American Imago,* 1960, *17,* 311–317.

Slaughter, F. Approaches to the use of music therapy. In E. Thayer Gaston (Ed.). *Music in therapy.* New York: The Macmillan Company, 1968, 238–244.

Smith, O. S. Music methods and materials for the mentally retarded. *Music Therapy,* 1952, 139–144.

Sparks, R. W., & Holland, A. L. Method: Melodic intonation therapy for aphasia. *Journal of Speech and Disorders,* 1976, *41,* 287–297.

Stein, J. Tempo, errors and mania. *American Journal of Psychiatry,* 1977, *134,* 454–456.

Stein, J., & Euper, J. A. Advances in music therapy. In J. H. Masserman (Ed.). *Current psychiatric therapies* (Vol. 14). New York: Grune and Stratton, 1974, 107–113.

Stein, J., & Thompson, S. V. Crazy music: Theory. *Psychotherapy: Theory, Research and Practice,* 1971, *8,* 137–145.

Toedter, A. D. Music therapy for the criminally insane and the psychopath. *Music Therapy,* 1954, 95–103.

Toombs, M. R. Dance therapy. In E. Thayer Gaston (Ed.). *Music in therapy.* New York: The Macmillan Company, 1968, 329–344.

Toombs, M. R. Musical activities for geriatric patients. In E. Thayer Gaston (Ed.). *Music in therapy.* New York: The Macmillan Company, 1968, 382–388.

Wasserman, N. M. Music therapy for the emotionally disturbed in a private hospital. *Journal of Music Therapy,* 1972, *9,* 99–104.

Weigl, V. Functional music with cerebral palsied children. *Music Therapy,* 1954, 135–143.

Weigl, V. The rhythmic approach in music therapy. *Music Therapy,* 1962, 71–80.

Weir, L. E. Merging the therapeutic and educational aspects of music. *Music Therapy,* 1955, 74–78.

Weisbacher, B. T. More than a package of bizarre behaviors. *Music Educators Journal,* 1972, *April,* 10–12.

Weisbrod, J. A. Shaping a body image through movement therapy. *Music Educators Journal,* 1971, *April,* 50–53.

Wells, A. M. Rhythm activities on wards of senile patients. *Music Therapy,* 1953, 127–132.

Wells, K. E., & Helmus, N. Music therapy for severe speech disorders. In E. Thayer Gaston (Ed.). *Music in therapy.* New York: The Macmillan Company, 1968.

Werbner, N. The practice of music therapy with psychotic children. *Journal of Music Therapy,* 1966, *3,* 25–31.

Wilke, M. The disc jockey jamboree. *Music therapy,* 1960, 47–53.

Wilson, A. E. Music in the treatment and education of emotionally disturbed children. In E. Thayer Gaston (Ed.). *Music in therapy.* New York: The Macmillan Company, 1968.

Wingert, M. L. Effects of a music enrichment program in the education of the mentally retarded. *Journal of Music Therapy,* 1972, *9,* 13–22.

INDEX